Simple Records...

John Ashworth

EDWARD'S GRAVE, Page 68.

SIMPLE RECORDS.

BY JOHN ASHWORTH,

AUTHOR OF "STRANGE TALES," "WALKS IN CANAAN,"

&c.

MANCHESTER:
TUBBS AND BROOK, 11, MARKET STREET.
LONDON:
SIMPKIN, MARSHALL, & CO.; HAMILTON, ADAMS, & CO.;
MORGAN AND SCOTT; F. PITMAN.

PREFACE.

ON looking over my diary for past years I find numerous notes, descriptive of scenes and circumstances, men and things, recorded at the time from a desire they should not be forgotten. Some of them entitled "Strange Tales" have already been published and have passed through many editions, and are now printed in many languages. Others are yet to follow. These simple records, consisting of twenty-four short sketches, are the gleanings of my diary, and should this little book have the universal and hearty reception given to my other writings, I shall be thankful indeed. I think my readers will understand my object in giving this additional volume to the world; I wish to do good, and I hope by heaven's blessing my desire will be accomplished.

JOHN ASHWORTH.

BROADFIELD, ROCHDALE,
November, 1871.

CONTENTS.

LITTLE SANDY.

———•◦•———

WHEN we visit a great and historic city it is
natural we should be desirous to see its marts,
monuments, halls, cathedrals, museums, and other
grand and celebrated institutions. Associations,
gather around many of them, all having their peculiar interest, more or less. But in order to obtain
a correct knowledge of these cities, not only of
what they have been but of what they now are
we must turn aside from the architectural to the
moral, from the inanimate to the intelligent, and
we shall then have a true conception of the really
important, and know more of what concerns us
most. In London, Pall Mall and Whitechapel
should be seen together; in Edinburgh, High
Street and Cowgate; the piled-up population of
the pent-up pest houses should not be entirely hid
by the gilded towers and marble palaces. Could
we dispose of a little of our starch, and our self-

B

elected importance, and turn aside into some of these back streets, dark courts, and moral gutters, and in a loving and Christ-like spirit mingle amongst the tatterdemalions, with the object of doing them good, it would make our manse or villa all the more beautiful, and touch a nerve of the soul that would vibrate with genuine pleasure; for

> How sweet the thought, that we may be
> A friend to some poor friendless one;
> For daily round us we may see
> Some suffering deeper than our own;
> To wipe a tear from sorrow's eye,
> Ourselves will feel the greater joy.

A humble, loving, Christian spirit amongst carls or kerns, is a grand security for watch guards, silk purses, or scented handkerchiefs, and a true passport to the affections of those whose love is worth winning.

It is well for mankind that ample evidence of these truths is daily to be found in many of our cities and large towns, and one of them we record with much pleasure.

"You are coming to the metropolis of the north; I should like you to see our dear boys before you return. I send you my card."

So said a letter bearing the Edinburgh postmark, and on my arrival in that city the writer sought me out, and explained more fully what he meant by " our dear boys."

God had greatly prospered this man, but he did not forget that it was God who had done it. He had a desire some way to honour the Lord with his substance, and personally labour for His glory, and the good of those who much needed help. Often when passing from his Gothic villa in the country to his place of business in the town, he saw what hundreds of other wealthy people may see,—swarms of the city arabs, ragged, dirty, miserable objects, prowling and howling at almost every corner, the pariahs and outcasts of society. Many of them were children left to run wild by their drunken careless parents; some of them youths— cunning, vicious, daring, a torment to shopkeepers and policemen; and all of them destined to become social pests or costly criminals, if some friendly hand be not stretched out to help them. It was amongst this class that David Harris began to work. Large and suitable premises were provided and furnished; and a general invitation was given to all the ragamuffins. Fifty-seven sat down to what they called " a tightener." Few of them could sing or say grace, but many of them could sing "Jolly Dogs." All willing were installed in their new home, and strange as it may sound, the new confederation was baptised "The Industrial Brigade."

These, then, were the "dear boys" mentioned in the letter, and with whom, according to arrangement, I was to spend a happy evening; but the demand on my time that day was so excessive, and having to speak on my "Walks in Canaan" in the Assembly Hall, at eight o'clock, I sent a message to the lads not to wait for me beyond a certain time, but go to bed, and I would see them as soon as possible. About half-past ten we drove down to the home of the "brigade." The little fellows had wisely been permitted to retire to rest, but the kind Christian governor and teacher was still waiting, and by gas and candle-light we inspected the washing house, kitchen, dining-room, school, gymnasium, and dormitory, all well adapted for their various requirements. Before entering the last-mentioned room, in which all the lads were sleeping, a short sketch of the lives of several was given me—one interesting young fellow was called Sandy.

Sandy was one evening sat on the lowest step of a seven-story house—cold, hungry, and dejected. He intended to double up in some corner of the winding stairs, and snatch a few winks of sleep before morning. This was the thirteenth night he had not been in bed,—the stairs, the manure boats on the canal, or some empty cart or old ruin, had furnished him with lodgings. For bread he had cadged about the streets, markets, or railway stations. His hair was matted; his clothes in tatters, and filthy; his hands and body the colour of mud. One of the boys of the new home saw his old companion in this state, and said,—

" Oh, Sandy lad, but ye do look dirty; canna ye ga hame ? "

" I ha na hame; mi mither is noo dead, an' mi father is nearly aye drunk; he kick't me out of the house, and I dinna ken whaur to go."

" Oh, Sandy, come gang wi' me, lad, an' I'll tak ye to the Brigade; they will scrub ye clean, an' gie ye clothes, an' food, an' bed; ye need only be good an' work, an' then ye'll be grand mi boy."

Sandy looked at the speaker, and saw he was now clean and well dressed. He consented to go with him, and on they trudged together to Leith-street, talking all the way about the wonders of the new house. He told Sandy he would now be almost a gentleman soon; that for four shillings a week he would have new clothes, a clean warm bed, good dinners, good school, and a fine playground.

"Do you pay four shillings the week?" asked Sandy.

"Yes; but if I have had a bad week, and not got all the copper ready, Mr. Harris will trust me; and if I get more money, he takes care of it in the bank; so ye see for four shillings we are all in a new, grand home. But we all go out to work at something, for he will not let us be idle, and that is a good thing, Sandy. You will soon be there now; and they will take all your dirty clothes away, and burn them—everything about you. Your cap, too, lad, will be put into the fire: they will have no filth in the brigade. Here we are, now; come in."

On entering the home, Sandy's clothes were all taken away and burned, and he was at once put into a large washing tub filled with warm water, and for once in his life he got a good cleansing. As he stood up to the chin to have the last swill, he saw his drunken father enter the door. He screamed out,—

"Oh, dinna come here, father; dinna come here,

oh, dinna, dinna; ye bruised mi mither, an' kicked me out; oh, I'll be happy here, father, dinna come here."

The governor met the father at the door, and urged him not to take the lad away, as he had so long neglected him, and he himself was seldom sober. The father growled out,—

"I heard he had got a shilling for carrying a box, and I came to have it."

The father went away, to the unspeakable joy of his terrified child; and Sandy got his new clothes on a clean skin, and then laughed and cried in turn—both laughed and cried for joy; and when he that night joined with all the boys in saying a prayer, and laid down in a nice, tidy bed, in white sheets and blankets, he cried again. The day following he got work as a message boy, preparatory to something better, earned four shillings the first week, the price charged for his food, clothes, washing, schooling, and lodging; the week after he earned sixpence more, which he put into the Brigade bank.

Having heard this about the poor child Sandy, I was anxious to see him, and pat him on the cheek. We then silently entered the large sleeping apartment containing many beds, and ample room for more.   The gas was partly turned down, and all was still.

Sweet sleep
Had rocked them all to rest.

With noiseless step we walked the broad aisle betwixt the line of beds, the governor and Mr. Harris in a whisper pointing out the various boys, telling me their names and trades.   That boy, said Mr. Harris, is learning to be a mason; that a joiner; that a tailor; that a telegraph boy; that a draper; and here is Sandy.   I softly stepped near his head, gently drew the corner of the sheet from his calm, beautiful countenance, and had the greatest difficulty to avoid giving him a little loving slap on the face. For several minutes I gazed on his thoughtful brow, and replacing the corner of the blanket, mentally, and not without a tear, said, "God bless thee, LITTLE SANDY."

NEW EYES.

———◆◇◆———

IF aught will bring down heaven's sunshine right
into the soul, and keep it there, warming and
cherishing the heart all through life, it is the con-
sciousness of doing good. Whatever the recipient
of our benevolence may feel, the instrument of
kindness will always have a thrill of joy, and the
force of that joy will be in proportion to the act
being willing, disinterested, and secret; for then it
partakes of the true nature of that charity that
hopeth all things, and never fails. Kind deeds
are the rich blossoms of a soul right with God, and
when the sweet scent and bright tinge is gone, the
fruit comes forth,—blossom and fruit both yielding
their reward. Many times have I seen this truth
illustrated, and the following is one:—

It was a cold, cheerless day in February; the
east wind had cleared the streets of loungers and
children; foolish people had crossed the middle of

the window sash with scarlet and crimson sand-
bags, called "Doctor's Friends;" the fireside was
the most attractive place, and few persons left the
house except on urgent business.   At one moment
the only life visible in one narrow street were a
blind fiddler and his dog.   The dog, as usual, was
tied to his master by a small chain, and the handle
of the little alms basket hung on his bottom jaw.
The man, with his face lifted up to the leaden sky,
and his sightless eyeballs rolling, was fiddling and
singing a foolish but then popular song, and the
sound was distinctly heard on many a hearthstone.
A shopkeeper and his wife had just finished
dining from pea-broth, veal and bacon, and what
was left still stood on the table.   The wife said,—

"No doubt yonder blind man would be right
glad of some of this warm pea-broth, and the poor
dog of these soft veal bones."   The kind dame at
once opened the door, descended the three steps,
met the shivering fiddler at the bottom, invited
him to enter, took hold of his hand to guide him the
way, and soon the beggar and his dog—the one
smiling, and the other wagging his tail—were
gladly dining at a warm fireside.

"Have you been long blind?" asked the good
lady.

"Fifteen years, ma'am; the small pox took my eyesight."

"And have you been begging your bread fifteen years?"

"No, ma'am; only a few years. I had two brothers that cared for me: they both died three years ago, and now I have none to look to me, and I was forced to go out to beg."

"Can you fiddle and sing any sacred music, psalms or hymns?"

"No, ma'am; I only know two, and they are both songs or ballads; an old sailor taught me both of them."

"But there are many nice hymns and sweet psalm tunes that would sound well in the streets. and bring more coppers into that little basket, There is a soul in sacred music that touches the heart better than foolish ballads."

"I do not know any hymns, ma'am; I wish I did."

"Well, then, while you are eating I will try and teach you one; and when you have done, you must see if you can fiddle and sing it, will you?"

"Yes, ma'am; I will."

The good lady then began to sing. She loved music, had a good voice, and often sang God's praises in the sanctuary. She sang with the heart and with the understanding also; and now with the heart full—full of love to her dear Saviour, and the poor blind fiddler and his dog—she sang,—

> "Not all the blood of beasts,
>   On Jewish altars slain."

The tune was one of those immortal strains which find an echo in the spirits of song, and lift the thoughts to higher spheres, to join the company of the harpers of heaven. It was that fine old tune called *Old Cambridge*.

The blind man, with his face towards the ceiling, rolled his now moistened eyeballs in evident delight,—even the dog seemed to forget his crumbs and bones, for even dogs like sweet music.

"Would you please sing it for me again, ma'am?"

Again and again she sang the tune and all the hymn, the blind man drinking in every word and every strain; and his dinner being finished, he took his fiddle, and, standing in the middle of the room, began,—

> "Not all the blood of beasts,
>   On Jewish altars slain,
> Could give the guilty conscience peace,
>   Or wash away the stain;

But Christ, the heavenly Lamb,
Takes all our sins away;
A sacrifice of nobler name,
And richer blood than they.

My faith would lay her hand
On that dear head of Thine,
While, like a penitent, I stand,
And there confess my sin.

My soul looks back to see
The burdens Thou didst bear,
When hanging on the cursed tree,
And hopes her guilt was there.

Believing, we rejoice
To see the curse remove:
We bless the Lamb with cheerful voice,
And sing His bleeding love."

Going through the whole, to the astonishment of the lady and the delight of the blind performer himself. After repeating it, in order to make quite certain, he prepared for leaving. His dog did not approve of this, but when he saw he must go, he looked up at the lady, wagged his tail, and seemed to say, " I shall call here again when we come this way."

On arriving in the street, he began the new music, with at least one interested listener standing on the top of the three steps. He acquitted him-

self well. On he went, until the sounds died away
in the distance. The new song of the poor dark
wanderer attracted considerable notice, especially
amongst his former acquaintance. The old sailor
who had taught him the two ballads was never
tired of hearing it: he rolled the quid in his mouth,
wiped his face, and declared it beat all the sea-
songs he had ever heard. They lodged in the same
house, and often when they were alone in the
evening he would say, "Come, give us a stave on
your squeaking cat-gut, and let us have 'Jewish
altars' all through; it softens my heart, and does
my old weather-beaten soul good." Nor was the
old tar the only one charmed with the new strain
and the grand words. Once the mother of a sick
son requested him to sing it under her son's bed-
room window; and many times the Sunday-school
children would join their voices with his, for they
knew both the words and the tune; and experienced
Christians would stand still to hear what they
knew to be a glorious truth. The dog had more
coppers dropped into the little basket he carried in
his mouth, and his master was able to get a warm
second-hand coat and a stronger pair of shoes. But
what was the most pleasing, the sublime yet
simple truths of the new song began to tell on the

conscience of the sightless musician. Like the old mariner, his heart began to soften. Often when he had finished his day's wanderings, bagged his fiddle, and was returning home, he would repeat the words over and over in whispers to himself.

Two months after the first call, a rather impatient customer scratched at the door at the top of the three steps. The moment it was opened, without being invited, he walked in, dragging his master after him. It was the dog, leading the blind fiddler. This time, a little savoury hash was given to one, and a good cup of tea to the other, instead of the soft veal bones and the warm pea-broth, as before.

"So you have called again to see us; and how does the new music answer?" enquired the lady.

"Well, ma'am; I do not know how I must tell you; I have no language that will be able. The day I called here—that memorable day—and several days following, I sang pretty well; but one day I could not sing at all."

"Why, had you taken a cold?"

"No, ma'am; I had a guilty conscience stained with sin, and the oftener I sang the hymn the more guilty I felt. The third verse met my case, and I was indeed a penitent. I remained in the house all day in great sorrow. My dog often put his paws on my knee, for he knows when I am in trouble. I thought the hymn over, but I could not fiddle, nor could I sing it. The last verse, led me to trust fully on Christ, and now I can indeed "bless the Lamb with cheerful voice, and sing his bleeding love." I have got new eyes; my spiritual eyes are now open; and I see Jesus, my Jesus, my Lord and my God. What a mercy I called here, and what a mercy you taught me that hymn. I was then blind both body and soul, now the eyes of my soul are open. I do not now walk in darkness, but have the light of life,—I have got NEW EYES."

THE THREE SISTERS.

THE history of almost any Sunday-school, if written by a faithful pen and loving heart, would furnish facts and incidents calculated to become a blessing to many, and especially to those who may have been at any time tempted to doubt their utility. There are few sights in this world filled with such thrilling interest as the gathering together of hundreds of children and youths, converging from various points to one attractive centre, and there mingling their sweet voices in artless hymns and sacred songs, and then kneeling down to implore heaven's blessing on the reading of heaven's Word, and asking for the presence and guidance of Him who never forgets the little children.

But the interest in these gatherings deepens when we reflect on their probable future. I well remember one Sunday looking on our crowded school in

C

Baillie St. with something like a spirit of prophecy. I saw it possible, that many seas would divide their future homes, and many trials attend their future lot; that some would, by energy, rise to wealth and honour, and others, by apathy, sink to obscurity; that paths of peace would be trodden by those blessed with early piety, and paths of sorrow by those found in the way of folly and gaiety; that the church would rejoice over some joining its ranks, and mourn over others blighting its hopes; that vigorous health and a long life would be the heritage of some, and feeble health and an early grave the inheritance of others. All, and more than all, that day predicted, has since come to pass; but in this short sketch we give only the account of one.

This one was, on the afternoon of that day, surrounded by twelve little girls, all greatly interested in something she was telling. At the request of the superintendent, she had left her own Bible-class, in which she was a scholar, to take the place of an absent teacher, and she seemed greatly to enjoy her new situation. She was one of three sisters, who had attended our Sunday-school from their childhood, and become members of the church. They were orphans, for their parents —Mr. and Mrs. Stott—had both died of con-

sumption, leaving their little ones in the care
of a kind maiden aunt; but as they grew up to
womanhood it became too evident that their parents
had bequeathed them the fatal legacy, for one by
one they drooped, lingered, and died,—first Betty,
then Nancy, and last Mary. But as they went
step by step to the grave—first in great fear and
tears, then in calmness and confidence—they taught
many around them that in Christ it was glorious
to die. Mary being in my class, and making her
teacher her confidant, caused me to know more of
her than her two sisters, though I often saw them
all. On the day of Nancy's funeral, Mary had a
strong conviction that she too was doomed. She
said,—

"I feel I must soon follow my dear sisters. I
know how they began, and have watched their
failing appetite, their constant weariness, their
sleepless nights; but for the sake of my kind,
patient aunt I will bear up as well as I can, and
work as long as I am able; but oh! it is bitter. I
should like to live. It seems hard to be cut down
when life's prospects are just opening, but I know
it will be so. Lord help me."

None but those who have passed through this
experience can form a true conception of the

anguish of that moment which reveals the fact that we must soon die, and especially to the young. The aged, feeble, infirm, and the miserable may hail the mandate of the last messenger: they are weary of pain and suffering. But the young, buoyant with joy and expectation, surrounded with merry, healthy, and happy companions, the pleasures of hope daily opening and brightening, these will join with Mary in saying, " Oh! it is bitter!" But the bitterness to Mary was not the fear of death, nor the fear of being eternally lost, for she had seen Betty and Nancy triumph over death, and she knew in whom they had believed, and she felt an unshaken confidence in the God of her departed sisters.

But at the time Mary confided her fears to her teacher, she showed no symptoms of consumption, and many thought she would escape the malady. Even her aunt had no suspicions. She was good looking, apparently strong, and always seemed cheerful; but a change came, for of consumption it may be said,—

" Thou hast no favourites; for the gay,
    The young, the rich, the fair, the brave,
    All find beneath thy ruthless sway
    An early grave."

The aunt was greatly distressed when her hopes respecting her last niece were blasted. She did all she could to save her dear adopted child; she was doctored, nursed, and taken to various places at the sea-side and in the country; everything possible in their circumstances was tried to avert the stroke. Her last sojourn into the country was to a place near Hollingworth Lake. I received a short note, requesting, if it was possible, that I would call to see her there. The day of my visit was a calm evening in autumn. She had been wrapped in a shawl, brought to the door, and placed in an arm chair, her head resting on a pillow, and her feet on a small buffet. The first glance told me her work was almost done. She requested that a chair might be set for me near hers. In taking her hand, I could not suppress my emotions. She saw this, and said,—

"Do not be sad, my dear teacher; you are looking on the happiest young woman out of heaven. I know in a few days I must sleep with father and mother, Betty and Nancy; but oh, sir, I have often wished I could have all the scholars in our school here that I might tell them every one how happy I am. I think every day now is as glorious as the day I found peace with God, through my dear

Saviour, and that was indeed a joyful day; and now again and again the raptures of that day are repeated by the constant presence of my dear Jesus. I now know the meaning of the words, 'joy unspeakable.' I have often sat here to watch the going down of the sun: there is something so grand in seeing him sink down behind the distant hills in a clear sky. My sun is setting, and setting without a cloud. I hear the shout, the song, and the merry laugh from the people in the boats on the lake, and the sounds of music from the shore, but it seems to me so empty and unreal. Oh how different from what I now possess. I often bless them in my heart, and wish they were all converted. But I never envy them. No, no! My joy is almost full, and my pleasures will never, never fade away." She then began to talk of several of the teachers and scholars who had gone before, and asked me if I thought she would know them again in heaven?

"Yes, I think you will. The hope of meeting in the other world those we have loved in this is one of those sweet thoughts that few would like to let die. It seems to me that in a future state our knowledge and conception of all things good will be expanded; and that we shall know many there we never knew on earth—patriarchs, prophets, and apostles; and it seems to me that pure and holy friendships formed in this life will not be broken off in the life to come. Pollok says—

> 'All are friends in heaven, all faithful friends;
> And many friendships, in the days of Time
> Begun, are lasting here, and growing still.'

One thing we know, that He who redeemed and saved us will be there in the midst of the throne, and that will be enough."

"O yes, indeed, that will be enough; He will be there, and lead us to fountains of living water, and wipe away all tears from our eyes; that will be enough."

These short but impressive observations were spoken in broken sentences, as her strength would permit. After a pause, she said, "We have often sung together in the class, and in the school: let us once more, and probably the last time in this world, sing again the praises of Him that washed us from our sins in His own blood." Her choice was, "Heaven is a place of rest from sin." When we came to the third verse,—

> "A life in heaven, O what is this?"

A radiance lit up her countenance that made her

look truly beautiful. She had her hands clasped, and her eyes fixed on the deep blue sky. I alone was singing. Her thoughts were too big for words : she seemed on the very verge of heaven.

It is impossible for persons in health and strength to realise the deep emotions of those standing on the verge of the world to us invisible, but to them almost visible. They are so near the scenes that absorb the entire soul, that their language seems to partake of the higher state of existence. So it was with Mary that day ; and, as she predicted, it was the last time we joined in song on earth. She soon went to mingle her voice with the great, grand chorus in heaven. The hymn we then sang together is now numbered amongst my favourite hymns, and when I hear it sung, my thoughts follow Mary and her sisters to those "depths of bliss unseen, unfathomed, unconceived."

THE NEW MOUND.

I HAD risen early, and walked from my temporary home at Pentre-Morgan, in Shropshire, to the old church of St. Martins, to witness a yearly custom or ceremony of which I had often heard, and in which I felt a considerable interest. It was Easter Sunday, the first Sunday in April,—one of those sweet, mellow mornings that seem to say, "It is the Sabbath of the Lord to-day." The sun rose without a cloud; his expanding beams bathed the hills and mountain tops with glory, gently lifting the soft gray mists from the sleeping villages, and gathering the dewdrop from the budding palms, the curling ferns, and the opening flowers. Birds of song hopped from their mysterious berths, and, shaking their wings, in notes soft or full, began their cheerful matins; and my soul, just then in harmony with the surrounding grandeur, said, "Surely God is here." Passing the neat almshouses, and opening

the principal gate, I entered the churchyard, facing
the steeple, beneath the giant arms of the tower-
ing elms, and walked along the narrow walks
skirted with the sombre yew trees. I then saw,
by the flowers neatly laid on several graves, that,
early as I was, others had been there before me.
Two persons were still there, silently strewing
daffodils, primroses, and sprigs of laurel over the
last resting-place of relatives and friends.

The soul's lingering affection for the departed is
the strongest link which binds the living to the dead,
for it is the heart that is the true embalmer, and
that longest keeps the precious features from decay.
The visible form which the affection may sometimes take depends to some extent on national or
local customs,—bronze, marble, granite, or plain
stone; the flower, the wreath, the evergreen, or the
weeping willow. Though offerings often indicating
social position, they are also of true love and real
sorrow; and whatever may be our nationality, or
the peculiar feature of our ideas, these monuments
impress the mind with a feeling not altogether
unprofitable. In a quiet walk in the public
cemetery, the old cathedral, or the ancient and
venerable churchyard, where the sires of many
ages sleep, we find many precious records, sug-

gesting thoughts and feelings it is well not entirely to forget.

One of the persons amongst the tombs was an elderly female, evidently poor, but clean and neatly dressed. The grave she was adorning was the resting-place of her husband; and she was arranging the flowers in the form of a wreath, so that the name appeared in the middle.

"This is a tribute of respect you are paying to some relative or friend, ma'am?" I observed.

"Yes, sir; and so long as my feeble feet will carry me to this churchyard, my hands shall spread flowers over this grave. Here lies one of the best of men,—careful, industrious, toiling hard for our bread, and always anxious that we might owe no man anything but love. I have shed many tears on this stone, but I sorrow not as those who are without hope. He loved his God; and for many years, as a lay preacher, he did what he could to tell sinners that Christ suffered and died for them; and I think he will have met some in heaven he was the instrument in getting there."

"Yes, yes," I replied, "it is indeed a great comfort, when standing beside the tomb of our loved ones, to feel quite satisfied that their eternal home is the home of the glorified. I am glad to hear you

say your husband was a worker in his Master's
vineyard : for his two or five talents improved,
he will have heard the welcome words, 'Well
done.'"

Amongst the headstones near the small gate
stood the other person I had first seen on entering
the burial ground.   Seeing I was anxious to learn
a little of the history of those sleeping around us,
he willingly rendered me assistance.   Pointing to
a vault near the church, he observed,—

"You will perceive that the stones of the tomb
under the yew tree have been recently disturbed.
The remains of Lord Dungannon have just been
deposited there.   It is the same Dungannon who
recently protested in the House of Peers against
bishops and clergymen preaching on unconsecrated
ground.   He had great power in this county, for his
riches were great, and his lands extensive ; I hope
he made friends with his ' mammon of unright-
eousness.'   There are no flowers on his grave yet,
but there may be during the day."

My guide then turned towards a new made
mound, saying,—

"It is with considerable pain I look upon this
spot.   These clods cover the body of one of our
Sunday scholars, once a fine, healthy young man of

much promise; one of those genial souls who made many friends, and of whom the church had great hopes; but he left his class before he was converted, before his heart was renewed by Divine grace. He thought himself too big to remain in the Sunday-school. He left the school and the church, thereby letting go the only tie that bound him to good things. He fell amongst Sabbath breakers, scoffers, and drunkards, and he drank to such a degree that life became a burden, and with his own hands he took his own life, and here he lies in the grave of a self-murderer. I feel much distressed on his account. Oh! that I had been more anxious about his salvation when he was with us, more in earnest about his real, true conversion, he might probably have then been brought to God, remained in the church and school, and thus have been saved. I fear I did not do my duty to him, and the thought troubles me now."

"He is not the only one of our scholars by many that wickedness has brought to an early grave," was my reply. "I have had much experience in Sunday school work, and I never see a boy or girl become slack in their attendance, but I fear for them; I know some evil influence is at work, which only requires time to bear fruit. We are told in the fifth of Galatians what that fruit is. A few months since I heard my name called out in the street; on turning round to see whence the voice proceeded, a young soldier came up whom I at once recognised as one of my former scholars, and one whom I had much difficulty in keeping to the school at all. He had given his parents great trouble, got himself into disgrace, and went into the army. He was nearly drunk when he spoke to me, but ' wished to have a word with his old teacher.' I think early conversion to God is the only guarantee for our boys and girls remaining in connection with the school and church, and we cannot seek for their conversion too soon, God can in some way unknown to us, adopt His saving grace to young hearts. The *child*, trained in the way he should go, will be an exception to the rule if he departs from it."

" What plan do you consider the most effective in securing their early conversion?" asked my guide.

" Well, sir, I think all classes ought to be taught in separate vestries : this gives the earnest, pious teacher a greater influence over his scholars. I had a kind, loving teacher, who took me and the other boys into a small, separate room, and many a time on the evening of the day, he would kneel down and pray for us, one by one, as our names stood on the class book. I have forgotten most of what he said to us, but not his prayers on our behalf. To pray for a child by name, and pray for his early salvation, must produce effect, and will ever be remembered."

We walked quietly through the whole church-yard, he pointing out the various objects of interest, and not the least interesting was a young mother, with a small basket containing flowers. We watched her pass down the avenue of small yew-trees, until she paused at the grave of her little child, and the sprig of myrtle, the primrose, the daffodil, were gently laid on the much loved spot, with a feeling that only mothers know.

I thanked my guide, and bade him good morning; but during that day, and many days since, that new made mound has followed me. The teacher's sorrow over the grave of the suicide; his exclamation, "Oh! that I had been more anxious about his salvation when he was with us," has rung in my ears; and I have many times resolved that my labours shall henceforth be for the early conversion of the young under my care. Minister or teacher, this is our true work : this 'neglected, little or nothing is done.   I had thought of this, and believed it before, but the conviction was deepened by that morning's visit to St. Martins.

A TROUBLESOME HALFPENNY.

TWO elderly gentlemen, talking about their early follies, each related an event still strong in his memory, and not likely to be forgotten. One of them said, "I will tell you how I was cured of the filthy habit of smoking.

"When I was an apprentice, I was sent to help in some repairs required at a large hall. I had just begun the foolish, offensive, and wasteful habit of smoking, to which all the men had been told the lady of the house had a strong objection, and to which I knew my parents had a strong dislike. One day, at twelve o'clock, several of us ascended into a large empty attic to have our dinners. Thinking I could have a smoke there without the lady knowing, I filled my fancy pipe, and opened wide a skylight to let the perfume escape. I had not puffed many times before I heard a clatter of feet, and a voice hurriedly calling out, ' Oh ! where is it? Where is it? I cannot find it in any of these

D

rooms ; it must be higher up.' And higher up the excited voice and feet came, and just as I had put the burning pipe into my pocket—for I had not time to hide it—in rushed the lady, exclaiming, 'Oh ! it is here. Pray tell me which of you have been smoking ? I am afraid of an accident by fire, and cannot do with the smell. Which of you is it ?' I held down my head in shame, saying,—

" 'It's me, ma'am ; I am rather poorly, and thought a little tobacco would do me good.'

" 'I am sorry you are not well ; get home as quick as you can, and go to bed ; you will perhaps be better in the morning.'

" Down stairs I went, not very like a sick person, for my fingers and clothes were burning, and I was in perfect agony. On gaining the outside I dashed my blistered finger into a pail of water, and poured a quantity into my blazing pocket, and then took to my heels towards home. My shopmates had many a hearty laugh at my predicament that day ; and years after, if any of them had been a little unwell, it was sure to be said, amidst roars of laughter, ' Get home as quick as you can, and go to bed ; you will perhaps be better in the morning.' That was my last pipe, and that was my adventure. What was yours ? "

" Well, sir, my trouble was not as hot as yours, but I think I was more miserable. When about seven years of age, I went every evening to fetch milk from a farm house called the Green. A prim, stirring, talkative old lady, named Matty, filled our pitchers. There was a low porch at the door, with a smooth stone table inside. On this stone we placed our vessels, and then waited until they were filled. One evening I was in the porch alone. There was a halfpenny on the stone; and while Matty was putting in my milk, I removed the halfpenny into my pocket. The moment I had done it I trembled from head to foot. When Matty brought my pitcher, I eagerly caught it, and away I went in great fear. On reaching home, I set down the milk, and then went into a field behind the house, in which there was a stone wall or fence, and walked the whole length of the wall to find a place where I could hide the halfpenny. I pushed it into a small opening with my finger, got a stone and put it over the hole to prevent it being seen; but all the while I felt that God was watching me, and that He was very angry with me. I returned home, but could not rest. I durst not look at my mother. I could not join in play; and I began to fear some one had probably seen me

hide the coin, and would find it and tell. I secretly
retraced my steps down the field, picked the halfpenny out of the hole, and buried it under a broken
flag behind our house. Again I feared I had been
seen, and again I removed it—this time under the
lowest stair in the pantry. All the time I thought
God was still looking down upon me, and grieved
with my conduct. Night came, and the time for
going to bed came; then my fears and troubles
increased. I durst not kneel down. I durst not
pray. I believed God would not hear my prayer
so long as I had the stolen halfpenny, and if I died
before morning—died with the halfpenny in my
possession—how could I go to heaven? Long I
stood beside the bed, not daring to kneel or undress.
At last I laid down in my clothes, and oh! what a
night! Heaven frowning, my mother weeping,
policemen, prisons, exile—all crowded round me.
I promised the Lord over and over I would take
the halfpenny back in the morning; and when
morning came, I rose early, found the terrible coin,
and ran as fast as I could run to the farmhouse.
Old Matty was in the porch, and I almost screamed
out,—

"Old Matty, old Matty; I took this halfpenny
off the milk stone yesterday, and I have brought it

back. Oh, will you forgive me, and not tell anybody?"

The old lady put both hands on my head, saying,—

"Johnny, Johnny; you were a bad boy when you took this halfpenny, but you are a good boy for bringing it back. I will forgive you, and not tell."

Then I began to be happy again: God seemed to smile down upon me. I durst look at my mother, and play with the boys, and pray when I went to bed; and many times since that day have I thanked the Lord for the tender conscience I then had, for that was my first and last theft, and the Lord still smiles upon me.

THE THREE TRUANT BOYS.

ONE Sunday afternoon, three boys, who were scholars in Bamford Sabbath School, played the truant. Without the knowledge or consent of their parents or teachers, they ran away from school. Some distance behind Bamford Chapel there is a deep ravine, which stretches for several miles. It is well wooded on both sides through almost its entire length. At the bottom of the ravine runs a brook. To reserve the water for the use of a small mill which stands below, an embankment had been built. The truant boys rambled on over fields and bye-ways, until they arrived at a place called Coal-Bank. They then rambled by the side of the brook, until they came to the reservoir, and sat down on its bank. A person who was passing by, told them that if they went into the water they would be drowned. Their answer was, "One drowned, all drowned." After sitting on the bank for a short time, they went in. Soon after, some one saw the clothes lying on the bank, but could see no one to own them. He raised a cry of alarm—people came from all sides—the reservoir was searched—and, at length, the three unfortunate boys were dragged out, locked in each others arms, quite dead. Little did they think that their answer to the person who had warned them of the danger was a prediction.

The report of their death very soon spread far and wide; it reached Bamford just as the congregation and the scholars were leaving the chapel, and painful, indeed, was the effect it produced upon every one. But, with the exception of their parents and relatives, none felt so keenly the sad end of those misguided boys as the teachers; these were sorely grieved, and one of them, John Crabtree, wrote a number of verses, suggested by the melancholy event—one of them we quote:

" The youths that we so much lament,
How unconcerned from school they went,
They did not death, nor danger fear,
Not knowing then, that death was near."

Numerous are the instances of Sabbath scholars running away from school, and meeting death in various forms. God's commandment, " Remember the Sabbath day, to keep it holy," cannot be disregarded with impunity. Accidents of various descriptions are far more likely to occur on the

Sabbath, than on any other day. Conscious guilt to a great extent, takes away the power of self-preservation, and when danger crosses the path, we fall before it, though at other times, we should have the power to overcome it. The Almighty has declared that the sound of the driven leaf shall chase the wicked, and that they shall flee when no man pursueth. There is neither peace nor safety to those who trample upon the ordinances of God, and the Sabbath is one of these. He instituted it in Eden; He threw around it the shield of His Divine Law on Sinai; He has never set aside the Law of the Sabbath, and until He does so, we can never safely violate it. Had these three boys attended to the instructions given to them in the Sabbath School, it is probable that they would now have been alive, and useful members of society; but, alas! they are laid in the silent grave. Melancholy were the circumstances connected with their deaths, and I trust they will be a warning to all boys who may think of running away from the Sabbath School.

> "In holy duties let the day
> In holy pleasures pass away;
> How blest a Sabbath thus to spend,
> In hope of one that ne'er shall end."

THE NEW SHAWL.

"MOTHER! mother!" exclaimed Jane Weston, "see what a nice new shawl this is; I wish you would buy it for me."

"The man has a great many nice things in his pack; but where is the money to come from to buy any of them?" replied the mother.

"Oh, I will trust you," said the packman; "you can pay me a shilling or two each journey, and I am sure you had better do so than let your daughter go without so cheap and handsome a shawl. I can assure you it is quite in the first fashion."

"Yes, the shawl may do," returned Mrs. Weston; "but you know we have one score on already, and I think we had better try to make it less than think of making it larger."

"That is the way you always go on when I want anything," said Jane; "but if I had as many fine things as some of our neighbours, who are no better off, you might talk about *scores*."

Jane's allusion to fine neighbours touched Mrs. Weston in a weak place. She had long struggled to be smarter than her circumstances would allow, in order not to be behind her neighbours; and had, in consequence, brought herself into unnecessary trouble. It can hardly be wondered at, that her daughter copied the example so frequently set before her. The shawl was bargained for, and the man added its cost to the old account.

Jane's appearance at the school the following Sunday, in her fine new shawl, attracted some little attention, especially from the girls in her own class. Some praised it, and asked her where she had bought it; some looked shy, and talked to each other in whispers; while some seemed really mortified, because she was finer than they were. Jane carried her head very high the whole day; but she little thought that this shawl would be the means of bringing her into very great trouble. One of her former companions lived in a small village, about two or three miles off. Though the wakes were held in that village that day, Jane set off, after the school had been dismissed, to see her. On the road she met with a girl going to the wakes. An acquaintance was formed; and she persuaded Jane to accompany her, during the following week, to one of the dancing-rooms. Those with whom she came into contact in this place, and the principles taught in it, soon destroyed all her affection for the Sabbath School. For upwards of two years she continued to attend their weekly meetings and dancing parties. Ministers of religion she learned to ridicule; the serious and thoughtful she called mopish and melancholy; chapels and Sabbath Schools, she said, were only nurseries of superstition; and those who upheld them did it for their own selfish purposes. But how true is the language of Holy Writ, "A prudent man foreseeth the evil, and hideth himself; but the simple pass on and are punished." Jane's gaiety and frivolity continued while her health lasted; but when sickness came, it wrought a very great change in her views and expressions.

She was attacked by a violent fever, and all who saw her thought that she was near her end. The nearer death seemed to approach, the greater her terror became. At her own earnest request, I was sent for. The moment I entered the room, she literally screamed out,—

"O, Sir, do come and pray for poor, poor me."

Her mother offered me a chair by the bedside. I sat down, and, after a moment's pause, took hold of her burning hand, and tried to speak kind and soothing words to her; but nothing would do but my kneeling down immediately, to pray.

"What shall I pray for?" I asked.

"O, Sir," she answered, "do pray that God Almighty would have mercy upon my poor, perishing soul."

I did as she requested, and she responded to my petitions with the most agonizing groans. When I rose to take my leave, she requested me to see the girl who had first persuaded her to go to a dancing-room, and entreat her to come and see her, that she might warn her of her sins before she died. She added, with a truly repentant look, "O that I had never left the Sabbath School; I should not now have been in this condition—there I did learn good things; but since I have only learnt to mock. O God, have mercy upon me!"

I saw her companion that day, and told her of Janc's condition, and how very anxious she was to see her. She only laughed at all I said, and, as I afterwards learnt, never went near the dying girl.

Jane Weston made a god of her dress, and this brought upon her trouble and anguish. To show her new shawl, though bought on credit, she went to the Sunday wakes; there she was certain to meet with the foolish and ungodly. Sinners enticed her, and sin plunged her into misery and sorrow; and she proved what all prove, that "the way of transgressors is hard."

"I'M TOO BIG NOW."

ONE Sunday morning, two boys applied for admission into our school. One was called Henry, the other Richard. They were nearly of the same age, and came from the same neighbourhood. After hearing them read, the superintendent put them into a Bible-class. For several months both attended very regularly. One Sunday morning, however, when the teacher was calling over the names, he stopped at that of Henry, and said—

"He does not attend so well as he did formerly."

"I have often called for him, but could not get him to come," replied Richard; "but I will call again this afternoon, and try to bring him with me."

When Richard called, he found Henry washing himself, and that he was going to put on a new suit of clothes. Henry's mother, turning to Richard, said—

"I hope my son will now go to the school regularly; he cannot, as he has done before, excuse himself by saying that his clothes are so bad; he has now got a new suit."

As they were walking along the road, Henry said—

"I will go to the school this afternoon, to let them see my new clothes, but I shall not go again after to-day: I'm too big now to go to a Sunday-school."

"Too big!" exclaimed Richard, "too big! why there are many boys in our school bigger than you: our teacher is much bigger; and you know he has often told us that he has never left the school since he first entered it as a little boy; and, as he says, if we leave as we grow up, what is to become of schools when the old teachers are dead and gone? You have often heard him say that we ought to pay back with interest what we have received to the next generation."

"You may say what you like," replied Henry; "I shall go no more after to-day."

He kept his word, for Richard could never persuade him to go again.

Now let us see what became of these two boys: Richard remained at school; soon became a teacher of a lower class; and some time after, of the first Bible-class. He became a member of the church; and the elders, finding him a pious, intelligent young man, promoted him to an office

of high trust and honour. After Henry had left
the school he began to keep company with a
number of young men who spent their Sabbaths
in sinful folly. He would sometimes remain in
bed until eleven or twelve o'clock on a Sunday.
He would then get up, and sit or walk about
until two or three in the afternoon. If he washed
and dressed himself, it was only to go with his
companions to some sinful place. Sorry I am to
say it, but he often helped his wicked comrades
to taunt Richard, calling him a mopish simpleton.

Several years rolled away, and in the meantime
both these young men got married.

One Sabbath last summer, Richard having to
preach in the country, took his little boy with him
for a walk. When they got near the chapel, they
saw a man lying drunk in the road, covered with
dust, and a ragged little girl bitterly crying by his
side. Out of pity to the girl, Richard went to lift
up the drunken man; but, what was his astonishment to find it was Henry.

My dear boys, when any of you begin to think
that you are too big to go to the Sunday School,
think of Henry and Richard; and how true it is, that
the beginning of sin is like the letting out of water.

"WHERE'S MY JACKET?"

"I WONDER wherever my jacket is gone; some of you must have taken it," said Frank Gee, while dressing himself one morning. "Have you seen it, Robert?"

"No," was the reply.

"Where can it be? I am sure I put it on this chair last night, and if some of you don't find it, you'll catch it."

"And you'll catch it, too," returned Robert, "for you have tumbled everything up and down, and lost my shoes: where are my shoes? Henry, have you seen them?"

"No," answered Henry, "I have not. Really, what a jumble you have made: you think about no one but yourselves, for I believe you have lost my stockings," shouted Henry.

'Hold your noise about your stockings, and find my jacket," called out Frank in a great passion; and at the same time he gave Henry a push, which sent him sprawling on the floor. Old Mr. Gee, hearing some one fall, ran up stairs to see what was the matter.

Frank said, " I've lost my jacket."

Robert, " I've lost my shoes."

Henry said, " I've lost my stockings, and Frank has pushed me down, and scratched the skin off my elbow."

Mr. Gee, hearing this, took Frank and gave him a severe flogging, declaring that the house was worse than bedlam every morning, through their shouts and noise about their clothes. Mrs. Gee, hearing her husband flogging Frank, flew into a great rage; and when he came down stairs, she told him he was not fit to govern a family, for he was always abusing some of them. This brought on a very unseemly quarrel between them, which ended by Mr. Gee taking up his hat and going into his workshop. When, about an hour after, his daughter Mary, a quiet girl of about sixteen, went to call him to his breakfast, he refused to have any; which caused Mary to cry. The differing of the boys; the sulking of the father; the scolding of the mother; and the crying of Mary, did, indeed, make the house as much like bedlam as it well could be; and all because

Frank and his brothers had carelessly mislaid their clothes when they went to bed the night before.

It is greatly to be regretted that scenes and consequences similar to the above, are so very common throughout the length and breadth of the land; and all through the want of a little order and arrangement.

I remember an anecdote, which was told in one of our schools, respecting four boys, who differed very much from the three before mentioned. The speaker had for his subject, "A place for everything, and everything in its place." After referring to various other matters, he said,—

" I am acquainted with four boys, whom I called to see the last time I was over in the neighbourhood where they reside. When I called they had gone to bed, and having to leave very early in the morning, I went upstairs to shake hands with them and bid them farewell. On entering the room where they all slept, I was struck with the order and arrangement of their clothes. They had each a large peg fixed in the wall, on which were hung, first the jacket, then the waistcoat, then the trousers, then the garters, then the stockings, and on the floor, just under the peg, a pair of shoes. When I expressed my pleasure at seeing their clothes arranged with such order, the master of the house told me that, though they had to rise two hours before daylight—it was then winter—they could dress in the dark, and without the least noise or confusion."

Peace can never dwell in a house where there is no regard to order. Where boys are in the habit of throwing off their clothes, some in one place and some in another, it is no wonder that some of them are found shouting, " Where's my Jacket?" Disturbance, quarrels, and confusion arise in many families, especially where there are several boys, all through the want of a little thought. Wherever I see this, I conclude in my mind, that they have no pegs in the chamber. What anarchy would these pegs prevent, not only among boys, but among men and women also. One half of the world seem to be without pegs in their chambers: they are for ever calling out, in some form or other, "Where's my Jacket?" These lost-jacket-men are very great disturbers. What a comfort it would be to society, if they would but get pegs in their chambers. The careless and disorderly not only make themselves miserable, but they cause others to lose *time* and *temper*, and

so make them miserable also. Let us all begin
to look after pegs, and when we have got them
put up, and things arranged in an orderly way
upon them, there will not be so many bawling
out, " Where's my Jacket ?"

SHALL WE EXPEL HIM?

———•———

THIS question was asked in one of our Teachers'
Meetings relative to a boy who had been a
source of much trouble; some of the teachers were
in favour of expulsion, others wished to try him a
little longer; and it was ultimately settled that he
should be continued another quarter; when his
teacher heard this decision, he declared he could
not continue to teach the class if that boy remained in it. On the following Sunday morning
the boy was removed to another class, which was
under the care of a shrewd but kind and benevolent man, who always received a new scholar in his
class in the most affectionate manner; in this case
he took the boy by the hand, and, in a friendly
way, bade him welcome, expressing a hope that they
should spend many a happy Sabbath together.
Two or three times during the day, the offender
attempted to talk to the boys on each side of him,
but was kept in order by the mild and soft, yet

firm, reproof of his teacher, who informed him
that, during school hours, all conversation must be
addressed to him.   He was now in a new element;
his wild and unsubdued spirit had brought upon
him severe and harsh treatment from every one,
both at home and abroad; against this his soul had
rebelled, instead of softening it had steeled his
feelings against both parents and teachers, and
given rise to the question, "Shall we expel him?"
But kind and affectionate treatment he could not
withstand; before the expiration of the quarter,
the lion had become a lamb, and to this day he is
in the school, and is now one of its most pious
and consistent conductors.

This is only one of many instances where
kindness has effected what severity had vainly
attempted. If the teachers' meeting had decided to
expel the lad, he would, most probably, not have
attempted to gain admission into another school,
but the link which bound him to social order
would have been at once broken, and he would
have been driven forth to swell the ranks of vicious
and abandoned outcasts.

We confess we are opposed to expulsions; in
the present state of things few cases can arise which
would justify having recourse to such an alterna-

tive. How dreadful must be the condition of a boy who is turned out of the house of moral and religious training, with the condemnation of hundreds on his head, subject to the cold and distant frowns of his old teachers, and to the scoffs and jeers of the scholars; where is his soul to anchor, or where is he to look for sympathy? It is very likely that, under such circumstances, self-respect will be destroyed, and then all hope is gone of his ever becoming anything but a curse to those around him. If we consider this well, we shall tremble for the consequences of turning any boy or girl out of our Sabbath-schools.

If we would take the trouble to ascertain the previous training and present circumstances of those we are disposed to expel we should generally find that they, above all others, demand our greatest sympathies, and most tender forbearance. Let this be given them, and by thus imitating the benevolence of our Divine Master, we shall have His blessing.

THE BROTHERS.

THE mother sits under the window at the end of the square table, making and mending. Five little folks are round the hearth, building wood castles, counting marbles, and repairing dolls. Little two-year-old Fred, the tyrant of all, and the pet of all, claps his hands because his elder brother had brought them each a nice, red strawberry, and all are elated, busy, and happy. The mother looks and smiles upon her precious charge, and, with a full heart, gives them her silent blessing; but the smile is somewhat checked by an involuntary thought,—What will you be, my children, and where will you be, in twenty years?

This unbidden question received a partial answer on the 12th of December last. In the postman's delivery that day there was one envelope, containing two letters,—one from an acquaintance, the other from a stranger, but both intended for me.

The stranger was the mother of the five children who, twenty years before, were building castles, counting marbles, and mending dolls,—the innocent, merry group which then, and not for the first time, received her silent blessing. The letter contained an earnest request that if I should visit a northern town to call at a certain number in a well-known street, and ask for her son, a miserable, wandering, wayward child, in great poverty and destitution, and try to do him good. That same week I had to pass through the town named in the letter, and I called at the wretched home of him who had given his family so much trouble. It was a common lodging-house, in a narrow, dark street. I knocked and entered, to the evident alarm of the stout woman who kept the house, and who suspected me to be a law officer on some disagreeable errand. But I allayed her fears by saying,—

"I am no policeman, mistress; I am a peaceable visitor. Have you a lodger called Fred residing here?"

"Yes, sir; I think he is out, but I will go and see."

She opened a door leading into a large room, from which came the sound of many voices. Fred was not amongst them, but one of the company engaged to find him. While search was being made, I said to the woman,—

"How long has Fred been lodging here?"

"About nine months, sir, on and off; he comes and goes, but is rather more settled than many of them."

"Does he say anything about his relations?"

"No, he is very silent; he seems to suffer much in his mind at times; no doubt he is starving. He got sixpence yesterday by getting in coals, and paid for his bed out of it, for he is very honest, but evidently a slave to drink."

Fred now entered. He was tall, straight, but poorly clad. He pulled off his hat, and took his seat behind the door, asking if I was wanting him?

"Yes, sir; and I shall perhaps best introduce myself by handing you this note."

He at once knew the writing, and took it with a trembling hand. The struggle to read it through was evidently intense. He held down his head long after he had finished it. He was fighting with his emotions, but they mastered him. He returned the paper, and with much feeling, and after several efforts, said,—

"It is from my mother."

"Yes; and you see she requests me to call upon you. I think you had better put on your hat, and we will have a walk. On gaining the streets, I asked him if he had any relations besides his mother."

"Yes, sir; one brother in this neighbourhood, in a respectable and rather high position. He resides in a country house, but his business offices are in this town. I often see him, but he takes care not to see me, though he makes a profession of religion, holding an important place in the church and Sunday-school."

"Will you show me his place of business, and I will at once call upon him on your behalf?"

He reluctantly consented, and, after crossing several streets, he pointed out his brother's establishment. I requested him to remain at a distance, behind a statue pointed out, and after the interview I would join him. He complied with my request. I entered through the glass door a rather elegant office, and was on the point of introducing myself, but the brother said,—

"I know you, Mr. Ashworth, and I know your errand. It is about my poor unfortunate brother."

"It is, sir; but how you know I cannot tell."

" Perhaps not; but I am glad you have called, though to me it is a very painful subject. The fact is, we have all done almost all we can, and my poor dear mother clings to him with all a mother's feeling. He and I were rocked in the same cradle, ate at the same table, went to the same school, sat in the same pew at church, and were trained by the same exemplary parents in holy precepts and excellent example. When about fourteen years of age, I was truly converted, and became consciously a child of God, and a willing servant of the church. From that day heaven seems to have smiled upon all my undertakings, blessing me in my basket and my store. About the same age my brother became very rebellious. He unwillingly attended church or family prayer; he went with foolish and ungodly companions; left home, and visited distant lands; then began to drink, sinking lower and lower. He returned, and we did all we could to reclaim and restore him. I bought him new clothing; offered him two pounds a week, with a promise to see him well established, providing he became trustworthy and steady; and gave him ten pounds as an earnest of my good intentions. He went into low company, drank the whole of the ten pounds, and sold the clothes off his back. I tried him again; appealed to him, for his mother's sake, to try and be a respectable man; but all to no purpose. I know he is shortening my mother's life, and this greatly troubles me, but what can we do?"

Yes, indeed, what could they do? Here was another illustration that one tale is good until another is told. Fred tried to impress me with the belief that his prosperous brother was indifferent, proud, and unkind. How many parents, brothers, and sisters would almost lay down their lives could they but reclaim the erring one. Nothing is spared so long as any hope of success remains; but when even hope is gone, and nothing remains but ruin and disgrace, it is indeed bitter. The brother promised to make him an allowance, to be given in small sums through the hands of a person known to us both. I then left the office, and found the object of our solicitude waiting for me behind the statue. He accompanied me to the gentleman selected as the medium of charity. The good man spoke words of wisdom to Fred, and promised to be his friend.

Several days after the interview with the brothers I received a letter from the mother, in which she said,—

"I had a letter from my unfortunate son, inform- ing me you had been to his lodgings, and had taken great interest in his welfare. Oh, sir, I do not know how to express my gratitude in terms sufficiently strong for the trouble you have been at in seeing after him. I do sincerely hope that the prayer which he says you offered up for him may not be lost, but that the Holy Spirit may operate on his soul, and that he may become a sincere Christian, and a respectable member of society."

May the mother's desire soon be granted, and her sorrow be turned to joy over poor, rebellious, wayward Fred. That "the way of transgressors is hard," and "godliness profitable to all things," is again verified in the history of these two brothers.

EDWARD'S GRAVE.

I ARRIVED one Saturday evening at a little town in the higher part of Westmoreland, and was informed by the coachman that there was no conveyance in the direction in which I was travelling until the following morning. I at once resolved to take up my residence at a boarding house until the following Monday; for I hold it to be the duty of every christian to travel as little as possible on the Lord's Day.

As I found neither the books nor the company in the house agreeable to my taste, I took a leisurely stroll through the streets of the town, to see, and as far as possible, to judge, the character of my temporary neighbours. As I was quietly walking through one street, I saw at the door of a house, which seemed to me to be the residence of a market-gardener, a little stall, covered with various kinds of flowers and plants; some with and some without pots, but all intended for sale. A clean and healthy-looking woman, who seemed to be the owner of the stall, held in her hand a small rose tree, which a young and pensive-looking girl, dressed in black, seemed wishful to purchase.

"Do you want it for yourself, Harriet?" asked the gardener's wife.

Harriet quickly drew forth her handkerchief, covered her face, and for some time stood silent, evidently weeping very bitterly. Harriet's sorrow affected the gardener's wife; for, though I had taken up and examined many of the flowers, she never seemed to notice me; but, stepping a little nearer the weeping girl, she again, but with a faltering voice, asked—

"Do you want it for yourself, Harriet?"

For some time Harriet was unable to reply; at length she sobbed—

"For Edward's grave."

This answer fetched the tear from the eye of the flower dealer, and with deep emotion, she requested Harriet to accept it as a gift. "I, too," she said, "would plant a flower on Edward's grave." Harriet took the rose-tree, placed it carefully in her basket, and walked silently away, for neither of them had the power to utter another word.

F

I must confess that I was much affected by the scene I had just witnessed. I waited while the woman had wiped away her tears, and regained her composure. I then requested her kindly to tell me the cause of the young girl's sorrow.

"I presume you are a stranger here," she answered, "or you would certainly have heard of the cause of Harriet's sorrow. Poor thing!—I am afraid it will break her heart. It is but one short week since she had a kind, affectionate, brother— her bosom friend, her constant companion, and also the hope and joy of his parents. Edward—for that was his name—had a comrade, who left this town a short time ago, and went to learn the business of a printer and stationer. Last week he came back to the town on a visit to his parents. A few of his old companions agreed to spend the Sunday on the lake, and they all strongly urged Edward to be one of the party. He told them that he did not like missing the school, and that he was sure his father would not consent. However, at their earnest entreaties, he ventured to ask his father's permission to go with them. The old man was deeply grieved at his son for making such a request. He pointed out to him the great sin of transgressing God's laws, especially by profaning the day which He has commanded us to keep holy. When the Sunday morning came, Edward set off to the school rather earlier than usual, in order to avoid meeting with the other young people. On the way, however, he fell in with three of them, who again urged him to join them. When he told them his father's answer, they laughed, and asked him how long he intended to continue a *baby*. Two of them came up to him, and each taking hold of an arm, tried to coax him to go along. with them, telling him that they could have a jovial day, and his father never know. Poor Edward was too weak to withstand their banter and coaxing. He went; and, having hired a boat, they spent the greater part of the day in sailing round the lake. At length a scuffle arose, in which they all took part. The boat was upset, and poor Edward and two of his companions found a watery grave. The old man has seldom spoken since his son was drowned : once or twice he has been heard to say, ' O Edward, Edward, could I but hope thy soul was safe! My child, my child, what has now become of thee ?' Beside yon steeple, which you see in the distance, his body is buried, and the white rose-tree, which his sorrowing sister has taken away with her, is to plant on his grave."

I thanked the woman for her kindness in relating to me the sad story, and returned to my lodgings deeply affected. The following morning, as the bells were ringing for service, I bent my steps toward the steeple she had pointed out. Among the numerous mounds, about the size and shape of coffins, there was one which had been recently made:—this was Edward's grave. Around the sides were planted a few white and red daisies, and at the head, the rose-tree which I had seen the night before. The loving hands of the sister had, no doubt, placed it there.

The services that morning were, to me, unusually solemn. On leaving the church, I turned round the corner, to take a last look at the mound; but, oh, what a sight was there. It was Harriet and her father. The old man rested one hand upon his staff, and the other upon the shoulder of his daughter. Big tears rolled down his furrowed cheeks; his bosom heaved with anguish; with trembling voice the old man said, "O, Edward, Edward, could I but hope thy soul was safe! What now is become of thee, my child?" The exclamation caused Harriet to sob aloud; and, not wishing to disturb their sorrow, I turned with deep emotion from disobedient Edward's grave.

How painful is the consideration, that few of our grave-yards can be visited, in which there is not some monument of early death in consequence of disobedience to parents, or the violation of God's commandments relative to the Sabbath Day.

Edward was not the worst of boys, he had many good qualities, and was much respected, and greatly beloved by his father and sister; it is a pity he disobeyed his parent, and left the school at the persuasion of foolish young men. And yet these examples do not seem to deter others from committing the same sins.

We hope the sad end of poor Edward will be a warning to all the boys of that town, and strengthen them in their determination to obey their parents, and keep to the Sabbath School.

THE WHITE FROCK.

"WELL, mother, what do you think?" said Sarah Spencer, as she returned from school one Sunday. "It is going to be our singing day, and we are all to be dressed in white; so I hope you will set about getting me a new white frock, that we may have time to bleach it, for I should like to be as smart as any of them."

"Well, well, Sarah, do not talk about new dresses to-day, for you know we have trouble enough about those things at other times," replied her mother.

Though Sarah left off talking about it that night, on the Monday she could talk of very little else; and, when two of her school-mates called to tell her that their parents had promised them new ones, she became more and more anxious for her mother to promise her; for Sarah knew that her parents were very poor, and would hardly be able to spare money for such a purpose; and when, on the Tuesday evening, her mother told her she could not buy her one, she fell a crying, and cried the whole of the evening.

Sarah's mother was very uneasy to see her in so much trouble; and, in order to get quietness, went, on the following day to a friend's, about two miles off, to see if she could borrow one which she had seen her friend's daughter wear, but it had been cut up, and made into a christening dress, for the little baby; this was a sore disappointment for them all, but to none so much as Sarah.

Sometime during the week, a neighbouring woman advised Mrs. Spencer to take Sarah's Sunday frock and shawl to the pawnbroker's, and get as much money on them as would buy the frock, adding, she had been forced to adopt that plan in order to get their Betty one; for, said she, if I had not done so, I never should have had an hour's peace.

"Nay," says Mrs. Spencer, "I think our Sarah would never agree to that." But Sarah called out that she would consent to anything rather than miss being a singer; and she not only allowed, but actually prevailed upon her mother to pursue that course.

Well, the singing day came, and Sarah, with a great many more, made their appearance in the school, clothed in white; and well do I remember the pride and self-complacency with which they looked round on the congregation. Some had on large glittering neck beads; some great black brooches; some had fans, and others smelling bottles in their hands. Some smiled and others coughed, that they might draw people's attention. Although the air was rather cold, the temperature of the room was anything but low. They were, also, for the most part, clad in lighter apparel than was usual, and therefore more exposed to the pernicious influences of a moist and chilly atmosphere. The result was that many caught colds, and one of them fell into a consumption, which, a few months afterwards, terminated her existence.

Sarah's white frock was of very little use to her after the singing day, but it was several weeks before her mother could find money to redeem her shawl and frock from the pawnbroker's; and during this time she was unable to attend the school, and this was a source of very great sorrow to her mother.

KATE.

ON the morning of the 15th of April, 1863, I
sent out several of my workmen to Crimble,
near Rochdale, and immediately followed after to
see each man in his proper place. It was one of
those brilliant mornings that make the trees, the
fields, and the hills appear to be tipped with gold;
the daisy, the primrose, and the early buds of the
hawthorn were opening out to catch the warmth
of the solar rays; the birds were chirping in chorus
from branch to branch, and the sweet warbling
larks were ascending with their melodies towards
the clear blue heavens, singing as only the English
lark can sing, and the thrush, from the topmost
twig of the tallest elms, vied with the lark in
slower notes but louder song. Everything above
and around was tinged with glory, and suggested
the thought of paradise.

I felt the influence, and in silent raptures joined
with David in saying, "All thy works praise thee,

in wisdom thou hast made them all; the earth is full of the goodness of the Lord;" but those sweet thoughts were interrupted by seeing in the dry ditch, near Woodgate, what I first thought was a bag of hay that some carter had lost. I crossed the road to be certain, and found it was no hay sack, but a miserable-looking woman fast asleep. My first feeling was to let the poor creature sleep on; but thinking she might possibly be wounded or sick, I stooped down, laid my hand on her shoulder, saying,—

"I think you had better not sleep here, my good woman."

She lifted up her head, looking wildly round; she tried to rise, but her weary limbs and sore feet made it very difficult; with a little help she got out of the ditch, but seemed quite undecided which way to take.

"Can you tell me the way to Bolton, sir?" she asked.

"Yes, you must turn to the left to go to Bolton. I am going in that direction, and you can walk on with me."

"And will you walk with me, such a ragged dirty thing as I am?" she asked, with great earnestness.

"Yes, I will walk with you, for you are my sister; we are all of one family, all brothers and sisters," I replied.

"God bless you for those kind words, for it is a long time since any one spoke kindly to me. Oh, how strange it sounds!"

As we walked on, she gave me, in short sentences, the following sketch of her sad history, taken down in my note-book at the time:—

"I come from Heaton, near Bolton. I will give you my name, but wish you not to tell it; they sometimes call me Kate. In my early days I was as happy as any young girl in Heaton; I then worked in the mill, and went to the Sunday-school. I began to keep company with a young man, and in our walks we often called at public-houses; one evening I was a little confused by having had too much drink, and though he had given it me, he spoke very sharply to me, and never came again; but I had got a liking for drink then, and for money to get drink I have been guilty of almost every sin.

"I am but thirty years of age; but I know I look more like sixty. I am nearly worn out, and feel I cannot live long; the last ten years of my life are like a most fearful dream; I have been

four times in prison, once in the madhouse, **mad**
with drinking, and once in a penitentiary; had I
remained there I might have regained my character
to some extent, for it was a good place, and the
matron was kind with me, and tried to do **me**
good; but my desire for drink was so strong, **that**
I ran away, and for drink went back to a life of
wretchedness. I often repented of my sins, and
many times wept bitterly, and then I got work **in**
the mills, determined I would do better; but this
did not last long, as I did not pray to God to help
me, for I thought I was so wicked He would not
hear me. I have wandered from place to place,
from town to town; for I was ashamed to remain
in Heaton. Last night I was wandering up **and**
down the streets of Todmorden, very hungry, and
without one halfpenny; and for fear of the police
I came outside the town, and sought shelter in **an**
open cartshed, but I durst not sleep, and **was**
afraid; for I am terrified when left alone in **the**
night, as most wicked people are. I set out **to**
walk to Rochdale, and have walked all **night.**
When I got to Rochdale, the six o'clock **factory**
bells were ringing; and when I saw the happy
young women going laughing, and some of **them**
singing, to their work, I sat down and cried, **and**

wished I was dead, and had no soul. Oh! sir, I
have often thought that to be an honest, industrious, virtuous young woman, engaged in useful
labour six days, and go to church and Sunday-
school on the Sabbath, is like heaven; and it is
heaven compared with my condition, for mine is
hell compared with theirs."

"How long did you remain in the madhouse, as
you call it?" I asked.

"About six weeks, sir; but I know nothing
about the first fortnight. When I came to myself
I felt very sore and very strange, but when I put
my hand to my head, and found all my fine long
hair gone, and my head as bare as the back of my
hand, I screamed with rage, but screaming would
not bring it back. I asked for a looking-glass:
they refused it at first, but when I got one, and
saw myself, I thought I should have gone mad
again; I was a fearful sight, I shall never forget
it."

"And you suffered all this through drink, did
you?"

"Yes, sir, drink began it. I never see a young
woman going with her lover into a public-house
or singing saloon, but I pity her. Young women
who attend such places little know what they are

doing, for many of them will find what I found, that those who take them in will be the first to loathe and despise them.

"I have now learned, when it is too late, that if a young woman wishes a young man to respect her, she must respect herself, and if she respects herself, she will never be seen in a public-house. It is no place for a modest young woman; she will not long be either modest or virtuous if she goes there. If I were the mother of ten children, I would rather bury them all while they were young and innocent than see or hear of them going to these wicked music-halls, singing-saloons, theatres, and public-houses; they are all bad, and all lead to misery and ruin. No tongue can tell the sorrow and suffering they produce in this world; it will never all be known, except in the world to come—and I often wish there was no world to come."

Kate was right here, as thousands know to their sorrow. Singing-saloons and music-halls are become sinks of iniquity, and certain it is that no modest young woman will ever be seen there a second time; but how often has the first time proved fatal to virtue and peace! Two young women, scholars in one of our Sunday-schools, passing by a singing-saloon one Sunday evening, heard the very tunes they had that day been singing in the school; they stood to listen, and a young man invited them to go in; they foolishly entered, thinking there could not be much wrong in a place where hymns were sung. Some time after an old woman came to my residence requesting I would go to see a strange young woman in a lodging-house, who, she said, " was weeping and fretting herself to death, and no one knew her." I went with the old woman, and found the poor creature in great trouble, with a child a few days old lying dead near her bed. I had the charge of her several days, and then got her removed to the workhouse; and this poor, weeping, heart-broken creature was one of the two scholars who had gone into the singing-saloon on that fatal Sunday evening, and there was made half drunk by a man who pretended to have so much regard for her that he would see her home; but soon after she had to run from that home to hide her shame, and almost die through neglect and want in a common lodging-house. She told me that the very name of a singing-saloon made her shudder.

I wrote to her father, telling him all about his lost child, of her anguish of mind for the disgrace she had brought upon the family, and asked him to take her back; but he replied that he durst not and could not take her home, but would look out some place for her. The letter was written with a trembling hand, showing the shaken nerves of the distressed father.

And it is no wonder his poor daughter shuddered, for these music-halls and singing-saloons are moral slaughter-houses, where everything good is destroyed; wicked men go for drink, and to find victims; and fallen victims go to take a terrible revenge on young men, for "their hearts are snares and nets." But what care the proprietors of these dens for the moral and physical havoc they make by their drink and temptations? Nothing; I believe that most, if not all of them, would sell our Sunday scholars, our young men and young women, to *Satan and perdition* for one shilling per head profit. The beautiful but miserably-disgraced stranger in the lodging-house, and Kate, the tattered, worn-out creature walking by my side, are only two of these victims; their names are legion.

I had now got to the end of my journey, and stood still to bid Kate good morning, telling her I was surprised she had not stopped somewhere in

Rochdale to get a little food and rest, but her answer was,—

"Yes, I have come through Rochdale, but I have my reasons for not stopping there. I am going to Bolton, to see if they will take me into the union, for I feel I shall soon die, and I want to die near where I was once an innocent, happy child. Oh! I wish I had died then, I should have gone to heaven then, but now I fear I shall never get there, heaven is not for such as I am now."

"Did you ever read the seventh chapter of Luke?" I asked.

"Yes, the latter part of it scores of times, but I always tremble when I read it."

"I am glad you tremble. Many drunkards, both men and women, are so sunk in sin, and become so hard, that they never tremble; they are past feeling. But I have hope for you now; I believe the woman mentioned in the chapter trembled when she came to Jesus, and Jesus never sends trembling sinners away if they come to Him."

"What you say may be true, but it seems too good to be true. I thank you for speaking to me, and who knows but Jesus may yet save poor Kate? O drink, drink, drink, what hast thou done for me!"

G

WILLY.

—⇥⇥⇥ ⇤⇤⇤—

I WAS taking a quiet evening walk on the sands at New Brighton, looking on the ever restless, mysterious ocean, and watching, for the thousandth time, with speechless awe and wonder, the gradual lowering of the grand setting sun, until he sank behind a sea of burnished gold; and, as the last ray of his glory shot up in the purple heavens, my soul said, Good night, thou emblem of duty. On retracing my steps, and when near the base of the lighthouse, three men requested permission to speak a word to me. One of them said,—

"We saw you in the assize court to-day; you are one of the jury. We have been two days waiting with great anxiety for the moment when the name of this young man shall be called. He is out on bail, and we are his bond."

The young man to whom he referred stood behind the other two. He had a pale and troubled countenance, and was evidently the subject of deep emotions.

"What is the charge against him?" I asked.

"Well, sir," continued the first speaker, "a few weeks ago it was Radcliffe Races. He went, contrary to his own conviction, the advice of his mother, and his old Sunday-school teacher, intending to see just one race, and return home early. Before the horses started, a young man offered to bet him five shillings a certain horse would win. Willy refused to bet; but the young man still teased and urged him to bet, until Willy lost his temper, and in his passion he pushed the man from him. He fell amongst some stones, the sharp corner of one entered the back of his head, and he died on the spot. An inquest was held over the poor lad, who was the only son of an aged father, a verdict of manslaughter was returned, and Willy was committed for trial to these assizes."

"What do you want me to do? A jury must decide according to evidence," I replied.

"Yes, that we know; but should anything be said against his character, we can assure you he is a steady young man. Until lately he regularly attended the Sunday-school, as a senior scholar and sometimes as a teacher of the children's class;

but, like too many, he left the school, and spent his Sabbath with careless youths in rambling about the fields and lanes, talking about pigeons, dogs, and horses. The lad who was killed was one of his Sunday companions. Willy's parents are in a dreadful state about him. Yesterday morning, just before we set out, two kind neighbours tried to engage the attention of his mother, until Willy should slip away unseen; but she heard him shut the back door, and followed us to the station, wringing her hands and crying out, 'Oh! will he ever come back? Will my child ever come back?'

"It would have been well if he had kept to the church and school, and loved and revered the Sabbath: the races would then have had no attraction, and he would have been safe."

Yes, he sees that now. When the judge arrived, accompanied with the high sheriff, and the sound of trumpets, Willy was terribly excited. He caught my hand, exclaiming—

"Oh! what shall I do? Oh! my poor mother!"

I thought he would have fallen to the ground.

The following morning at nine, all the jury had assembled in the criminal court. My name was called the first, and I had to serve that day.

About eleven, Willy's case was called. He stood up, pale as death. The judge looked at the calendar. The crier, as usual, said, "Prisoner at the bar, do you plead guilty or not guilty?"

Willy tried to speak, but could not. All eyes were upon him, and all seemed to feel for him. Everything was said that could be said in his favour, but there could be no question about the verdict. That he had killed—but unintentionally killed—the young man there was no doubt. The sentence was pronounced, and in words of tenderness the judge expressed his regret that Willy had not kept to the church and Sunday-school, for had he done so, the lad now dead might have been still living, and the prisoner might have been a happy young man.

Willy, like all who turn their backs on the house of prayer, left "the path of uprightness to walk in the way of darkness." Did they but keep to the school, the house of prayer, and love the Sabbath, then should they walk in their way safely, and their feet should not stumble.

LUCY SMITH.

THERE lived in our village a poor woman, whose two daughters, Lucy and Ellen, attended the Sabbath-school. This poor woman, like many others, was unable to get those things for her children, which one of them at least thought she should—for children are sometimes unreasonable, and want things which their parents cannot get for them. "What," exclaimed Lucy, on entering the house one Sunday noon, "nothing but that for dinner; you never get us Sunday dinners like other folks; before I will have that I will be without;" and she sat down in one corner sulking. "Well, Lucy," said her mother, "I have got you all I could, you know I have not much coming in to get you a dinner with, if I could get something better, I am sure you should have it; I had your shoes to pay for last night, and a cap for Robert to begin going to school in, and I have many other things to do which you don't seem to think about; I dare say I could have had something from the grocers on trust, but that would be running into debt." "You always talk in that way," said Lucy, peevishly, "if I have had new shoes I work for them." " But neither you nor I get much wage," said Ellen, "and I am sure mother does as well as she can." "Who spoke to you? mind your own business," replied Lucy, angrily. " O Lucy, Lucy," said her mother, while the tears rolled down her face, "you little know how you distress me by behaving as you do, and making us all uncomfortable." " Hush, mother, don't cry," exclaimed little Robert, "when I get a big boy I will get you a great deal of money, and then we can do without sister Lucy, cannot we, mother?" Lucy rose to give her little brother a blow, but his mother slipped in between, and put her back. Lucy took her bonnet and went out in a pet, shutting the door violently after her.

Now, my dear young girls, whether do you think Lucy or Ellen would be happier at the school that afternoon? Lucy could not be happy, for it is in the very nature of things that those who make others miserable should be miserable themselves. Suppose when Lucy went home she had said, "Well, mother, you have not a very fine dinner to-day, but it might have been worse, for I dare say there are thousands without any dinner at all, who would be glad to sit down and take a little with us, and it is much better to have plain than fine dinners for which we should have to run in debt. Come, Robert, put your hands together and let us ask God to bless and sanctify it to our use." How happy she would have been herself, and what pleasure she would have given to her poor mother, sister, and brother.

You may see from this short but true story, how much sorrow one little girl may be the means of causing in a family; and I hope our scholars will avoid such conduct under all circumstances, remembering the fourth commandment,—" Honour thy father and thy mother."

A MISTAKE.

———o———

A CLEAR conscience is a sweet, pleasant, cheerful companion—one we can live with, sleep with, talk with, or walk with. It makes the face placid, the nerves firm, and the heart bold; it dreads no foe, it knows no fear, and is tranquil amidst darkening clouds and gathering storms. But a guilty conscience—a conscience laden with crime, secret or known—is a restless, perpetual torment. It is fearful, craven, cowardly, and destitute of peace. David, though a king, quailed before the reproof of the prophet Nathan; the handwriting on the wall struck terror to the heart of Belshazzar; and Peter, from his Master's look, went away in trouble to find a place to weep. They all knew they were guilty, and it was this conscious guilt that made them dumb and rendered them powerless. But it is a mercy that God has implanted in the soul this silent monitor, given us this faithful friend to warn us from the door of sin. If we give ear to the warning, and, like Peter, seek a place to weep, it is an evidence that the conscience is not yet seared, and that pardon is near at hand. The following case may better illustrate my meaning :—

A young woman, well and neatly dressed, and whose conversation indicated that her education had not been neglected, sought a private interview, in order that she might lay before me the cause of her daily sorrow, and ask for advice. After many efforts to speak, she said,—

"For fifteen months I have kept a matter secret that hourly becomes a greater burden to bear. It is about one year since I held a responsible situation in a wealthy family. One morning, I saw the youngest child playing with a gold trinket; I took it from the child, intending to restore it to the place it belonged. Instead of doing so at once, I put it in my dress pocket, until I went upstairs. In the evening I changed the dress, and for several days did not put it on again. About four days after, I was greatly alarmed by meeting on the stairs one of the servants, who told me, with much indignation, that the master and mistress had ordered them all into the breakfast-room, to enquire after the missing trinket, and had talked as if some one of them had taken it. Had she not passed me hurriedly, she must have seen the change that came over my countenance; for I felt as if all the blood had left my body, and it was with great difficulty I could walk into my room and shut the door. For the greater part of an hour I felt stupified, and could scarcely tell what I was doing. 'What shall I do?' I over and over again asked myself. 'Shall I take the thing at once, and tell them the plain, simple truth? Shall I do right, and take all consequences?' Oh, I now wish I had done so that minute. Had it been some ladies, I no doubt should have done so; but the mistress was cold, distant, and suspicious, and might not believe me; and the very thought of being suspected of dishonesty was dreadful, for others that I loved dear as my life would be involved in the disgrace. My parents were persons of high moral character, and had brought up their seven children with great patience and care; and to have one charged with doing anything wrong, would have been a sad blow to all. I shall never forget that fearful night. I know not whether I slept at all. I saw myself turned out of the house with loss of character, all my future prospects blasted, and our family brought to shame on my account. This I was determined should not be, if I died of the secret; so the following morning, having to go to the draper's, I took the trinket with me, and dropped it down an iron grate into the deep sewer."

The last sentence, "and dropped it down an iron grate into the deep sewer," was spoken in almost a whisper. She knew she was confessing to a foolish action, and a great mistake, and found it difficult to speak the words. It was a pity she had not more confidence in her mistress, that she could not frankly and safely tell her the plain truth; others would then have escaped suspicion, and fifteen months of pain of mind been prevented. Some good ladies know that if they must live in large houses, keep carriages, and receive company, they must have servants to help them; and feeling that there is a mutual obligation, they are courteous and kind, taking an interest in all that concerns the servants' welfare. The result is they are loved, cheerfully obeyed, and seldom change. I have this week been the guest of a gentleman who wished to introduce a servant to me, one that had been with them forty five years. On one occasion when his lady was stepping into her carriage to go out, one of the servants told her she wished to give a month's notice. "Wait until I return and then I will speak with you," was the lady's answer. When she came back she called the servant and requested to know her reasons for giving notice to leave. "Do you want more wages ?"

" No, ma'am."

" Are you short of good food, or do you want to change ? "

" No, ma'am."

" Am I and the master and children not kind to you ?"

" Yes, ma'am, you are kind."

" Well, then, what is it ?"

" The cook says she will slap my face, ma'am."

The cook was called in and informed of the charge against her. She burst out laughing, and protested it was all a mere playful joke.

" Now you see, if I had taken your notice to leave, I should have been as foolish as you ; and I will notice you if you give me notice again."

It is six years since this took place, and the servant and mistress are still very good friends. Had the poor trembling creature lived in that house, she would not have dropped the trinket down the grate.

" How was it you were not summoned into the

breakfast-room, along with the others, to answer about the lost trinket?" I asked my visitor.

"Well, sir, I was in a different position—regarded more as an equal than a servant. I don't think I was suspected."

"That fact would have made it easier to confess and explain the matter to your mistress."

"Yes, I see it now, and see the great mistake; but it is done, and cannot be recalled. I have known little peace since; that trinket down that grate is constantly before me. I cannot join in cheerful company; I cannot read. I am regular at the church and other means of grace, and willingly and painfully join in the confession of sins; but I have a constant impression that I ought some way to acknowledge my fault, and make restitution, before I can hope for pardon and peace. But I have kept it pent up in my breast, like a fire, until I can keep it no longer. You are the first I have told. I see from your writings that you have to advise in all manner of cases, and now, please tell me what I must do?"

"Was the trinket some antique article, valuable beyond its intrinsic worth, a precious family heirloom?" I asked.

"Oh no, sir; it was nearly new, and a very

common pattern. Most jewellers sell them; the price might be about twenty-five shillings."

"I am glad to hear you give that answer, for it makes restitution possible and easy. There are some sins against God and our fellow-creatures of a nature that make restitution impossible, but this is not one. It seems that your wisest course will be to purchase one, the exact pattern of the trinket down the grate, and return it at once."

"But how must I send it?"

"Enclose it in a parcel, with a note, stating that the trinket was not stolen but kept in a mistake, for which you are very sorry."

"But must I sign my name? I dare not. They will know my handwriting. I know the lady so well, I fear she would not believe me."

"It would be better if you could sign your name; but if you dare not, I will write the note for you, and you can post it from some neighbouring town, and they will get their own, or an equivalent, again."

"Oh, thank you, thank you; I will do it this day. I already feel a comfort to which I have been a stranger this fifteen months, and I feel I can now be cheerful, social, and happy again. Oh! what I have suffered. I durst not pray, for I thought God was angry and would not hear me. He will hear me now."

"Yes; and when you are again tempted to do wrong—as you no doubt will be, for we all are—ask the Lord to guide and strengthen you to do right. You are no thief; you did not steal the trinket, but you destroyed it, or purposely lost it; and your conscience condemned the act, and rightly so. But in your future times of perplexity, seek Divine direction in prayer, and you will probably be saved from many a sin and many mistakes."

OLD THOMAS.

NO doubt many in this neighbourhood will remember that at the Middleton Junction, betwixt the main line and the Oldham branch, there was a small plot of ground, in the form of a triangle, kept in neat order and well cultivated. A ruddy-faced, white-haired, healthy and respectable old man named Wright took great pleasure in dressing this precious piece of land, causing it to bring forth fruit abundantly. Being at the station, and finding I must wait an hour for the train, I descended the bank, entered the garden, and requested the aged husbandman to allow me to render him a little help. He smiled, found me a weeding hook, and set me to work. Thinking I could learn something from one so venerable, I said,—

"I think the soil is very grateful, if well cultivated. We read of it paying thirty, sixty, and one hundred per cent., and that is good interest."

H

"There is no telling what it can do," he replied. "I take a thimbleful of radish seed, drop it in the prepared ground; it comes forth, rears its head, until it covers my wheelbarrow. I sow a pinch of lettuce or rhubarb seed; it springs up and spreads out almost as big as an umbrella. It is wonderful to watch the daily opening and expanding of sweet-scented flowers: the variety, colour, and form of plants is amazing. God indeed has given us all things richly to enjoy, and all His works praise Him, and His saints bless Him."

"That is true, my friend; there are nearly two hundred thousand plants, all different, all beautiful. and all wonderful. I am pleased with your reply, especially the latter part of it. How long have you seen God in His works, and blessed Him?"

"I have seen Him in His works, and felt Him in His Word, sixty-four years, and I see Him and feel Him more and more daily. I am a very happy man, sir."

"I wish you would tell me how you began to be happy."

"Well, sir, when I was sixteen years of age, one hay-time, my father sent me to the village smithy, to have the hay-fork sharpened. The blacksmith had a large piece of iron in the fire, and he said, 'My lad, I want you to take hold of the big hammer, and when I take this iron out of the fire give it five or six blows : I will strike first, and then you; and when I ring my hammer on the anvil you must stop.' I took hold of the hammer, rather proud of my job, and he took the white fizzing iron out of the fire, dashed it on the anvil, gave it a blow, and I gave it another. The third time, I missed the hot iron and struck the anvil, making it ring again, and I was so vexed at the mistake that I swore. He stopped striking, put the metal back into the fire, and, looking me right in the face, said,—

"'Why, my lad, you have sworn. I wish I had not asked you to strike for me, you have sworn, taken God's name in vain. I am very sorry I asked you to strike, very sorry you have sworn.' Stepping to the door, he called out, 'Mary.' A middle-aged, cheerful-looking woman answered, 'Yes,' and came into the workshop. The smith said to her, 'Mary, this boy has been swearing. He came to have the pitchfork sharpened. My striker not being at hand, I asked him to give the bar a few blows : he struck right twice, missed the third time, and swore. I am very sorry I asked him to strike for me. I will sharpen his fork, and let him go.' The woman, putting both hands on both my shoulders, said,—

"'And did you swear, my boy? Did you take God's name in vain? I, like my husband, am sorry. We never swear here, and it gives us pain to hear others swear. We love God, and revere His holy name. You will not swear again, will you?'

"I tried to say 'No' to the woman, but could not, for I felt as if I should choke. I saw I had done wrong as I had never seen it before. I felt ashamed and disgraced. She saw my confusion, and not wishing to distress me further, she led me to the door, pointed to a small school-room in the distance, and informed me there was a religious service there every Tuesday evening, and that she and her husband would be very glad to see me attend the following Tuesday.

"My fork, being now sharpened, was handed to me. I laid it across my shoulder, and set out for home. But I was in great trouble; I knew I had sworn many times before that day, and now saw it a great sin. I told no one about what had taken place at the smithy. I did not promise the woman I would go to the Tuesday evening service, but inwardly vowed I would. The night came, and in great fear I went. The blacksmith and his wife were both present, and greatly pleased to see me. The service that night was heart-searching and impressive. The two following days I spent several hours in the barn and fields, reading the Scriptures and praying for pardon. The third day I found peace by believing on Christ the Son of God; and here I am, eighty years of age, and sixty-four of those years I have been a member of the church, doing a little in the Sunday-school; and, as I said before, I am very happy. I have often been thankful I took the fork to the smithy; it was a good day for me."

"Do the good blacksmith and his wife still live?"

"No, they are both gone; they died in great peace, full of years, and greatly respected. They did much good in their time, and now 'their works do follow them.'"

The small piece of land at the junction now lies waste. The venerable husbandman, who so much interested me that day, has laid down his spade. According to his own testimony he was happy here, and I think he is not less happy now. Should he have met the good blacksmith and his wife in heaven, it is possible they may have said something about the day Thomas went to have the hayfork sharpened, and what followed.

RACHEL RILEY.

—◦◦◦—

AMONGST the fourteen or fifteen girls who formerly composed my class, there was one, now no more, who often arrested my attention. She was a quiet, subdued girl, about fourteen years years of age, dressed in a black willow bonnet, blue printed frock, white pinafore, and a little drab shawl: her name was Rachel Riley.

Young as Rachel was when called away, her cup had been a bitter one, in consequence of the misconduct of a drunken father, whose intemperance and neglect of work often reduced his family to the most painful poverty and trying difficulties, and had it not been for a virtuous mother, whose affectionate sympathy often wiped away the falling tears, her cup would have been more bitter still.

Rachel's mother became converted soon after she was married, and her attachment to the house

of God brought upon her severe persecution from
her husband, especially when he was intoxicated.
Returning from the public-house on one occasion,
and finding she was gone to her class, he com-
menced storming and raging in the most violent
manner, threatening vengeance on every one about
him; after his rage was spent, he sat down and
fell asleep. Rachel, as she had often done before,
wept bitterly, and when she saw her father was
asleep, she went as quietly as possible to the door
to look out for her mother; when she saw her
coming, she went to meet her, but when she
attempted to tell her how her father had gone on
she could not speak for crying.

"Come, come, Rachel, dry up your tears," said
Mrs. Riley, "I see how things are. I have given up
attending my meeting once or twice for quietness,
but there was always something else found as an
excuse for storming. Our place is to do our duty,
and give no just cause for these scenes; but if
father will not go with us to heaven, we had better
not go with him to hell."

"But do you not think, mother, that he may yet
find mercy? When I think of him being lost I
sometimes feel as if my heart would break."

"My child, thy father's salvation has been the

burden of my prayers for many years, and I hope that he will yet see the error of his ways."

On entering the house, Rachel took off her shoes and went upstairs to bed, but her deep sorrow and concern for her father kept her long awake, and many a prayer that God would have mercy upon him ascended from her afflicted soul.

It was about this time that I missed her from school, and on my calling to learn the reason, I found her evidently in a rapid consumption. She expressed her joy at seeing me, and requested me to take her library book and return it, adding, with deep emotion, "I shall never come to school again."

"O Rachel, my child, whatever do you say," exclaimed her mother, "you must not say so; I cannot bear to hear you talk of dying."

"Mother," calmly replied Rachel, "I know your troubles, that they are many and grievous, and I did not want to increase them by telling you how very ill I am, but I cannot long deceive you; I feel my time on earth is very short; my prayers have been many that for your sake I might be spared, but I feel it must not be so. Weep not for me, mother, for who knows but that Being who is too wise to err is taking me from the evils to come. You know, mother, you cannot mourn for me as one without hope; no, no, I am going to heaven. You may struggle in the wilderness a little longer, but I know you will soon follow me; and, if God will permit, I will be one of the angel-host to bear your happy spirit to the skies; then, mother, our tears will be for ever wiped away. But, oh! my father, what will become of him?" As she mentioned her father, she laid her head back in the chair, and big tears rolled down her cheeks.

While Rachel was speaking, Mrs. Riley buried her face in her hands, and cried like a child. I could not speak, and for some time we all gave vent to our tears. Rachel first spoke, and asked her not to forget the promise which assured her that all things work together for good to them that love God; and, turning to me, requested that I would join her in singing her mother's favourite hymn, adding, we may perhaps never sing together again until we join the happy choirs above. She handed me her school hymn book, and pointed to the beautiful hymn—

> " When I can read my title clear
> To mansions in the skies."

I fixed on a tune she loved, called Burnett.

The fiery eloquence of her eye, her clear though feeble voice, the glowing rapture that beamed on her whole countenance as she uttered the two last lines of the first verse, showed a soul unspeakably happy; it seemed as if heaven, with all its glories, was opened to her view. I felt much difficulty in singing, my emotions frequently overcame me; her mother could not join us until we came to the last verse, and then her voice was low and tremulous. When the hymn was finished, she requested me to pray with her, adding, and do not forget my father. On taking my leave, she begged I would give her love and thanks to all the teachers, and tell her class-mates to meet her in heaven.

Never shall I forget the sweet solemnities of that hour; angels of love seemed to be hovering around us, imparting joys which none but those who dwell in Christ can know.

That evening Rachel took her bed, and to all it was evident she was fast hastening home. The day before she died she sent for her father; when he entered the room, she fixed on him a look of melting tenderness. "Father," said she, "I am going to leave you, and, oh, I fear it will be for ever. I have one request to make before we part,—dear father, will you grant it?" The tear stood in his eye as he replied,—"What is it, Rachel?" "Father, dear father, will you meet me in heaven?" This request touched his heart, and with quivering lips he answered,—"I will, my child." Then presenting to him her school hymn book, she replied,—"O God, grant it may be so."

The following day she breathed her last, and now she is gone to where

"No wave of trouble rolls
Across her peaceful breast."

YOUNG PHILIP.

SIXTEEN fine lads constituted our Bible class, seven of whom had modestly, but firmly, made an open profession of religion, and daily gave evidence of their true conversion. Six of them are yet happy, hard workers in the Church, instrumental in doing much good, respectable, respected, and prosperous men; proving that godliness is profitable for all things. Of the seventh lad, Philip, we have a few words to say.

He was the worst dressed boy in the class, but always clean, making his threadbare garments look as well as possible. He could not raise the money for a pair of shoes, but he kept his clogs well brushed and as bright as possible ; he attended the school so regularly that the first time he was absent became a subject of observation. On the third Sunday, a little girl came up from one of the lower classes, to tell us that Philip was ill, and wanted us all to go and see him. After school

hours the teacher and eight of his pupils set out
to see their sick friend; they found him in the
third storey of an old brick house, overlooking
the river Roach, in a locality called Dunkirk.
The bed on which Philip lay, was like his clothes,
poor but clean; the room was large, open to the
rafters, having been formerly used for flannel
weaving, and was without any furniture, not a
table, stool, or chair. As we one by one gathered
round his bed, hat in hand, Philip's pale face became flushed. To relieve him I said,—

"We did not know you were so poorly Philip;
we have come straight from the school to see you.
A woman below, I suppose your mother, informs
us you have been confined a fortnight."

"No, sir," said Philip, "she is not my mother;
my mother died when I was a child, and I never
knew my father, I am what they call an unfortunate child. In my early days I was sent to
the coal-pit, and there suffered much hardship
and great privations; for several years I have
worked in the mill, but have had no settled home.
I am in poor lodgings now, but I shall not be
long."

A quiet smile played on his wan countenance
as he uttered those last words; that smile told its

own tale, he knew he was dying, and he knew he was going to his Saviour.

"I am so pleased you have come to see me. You little know what a joy it is to look on my teacher and classmates once again; oh, that Sunday school, that blessed Sunday school! It has been to me the bright spot of my existence. There I found peace with God, through my Lord and Saviour Jesus Christ. I cannot tell you with what pleasure I have hailed the Sabbath morning, and with what rapture I have joined in singing the hymns. Three weeks since to day, we sang, 'The voice of free grace cries escape to the mountain,' ending with 'Hallelujah to the Lamb who has brought us a pardon;' it seemed to me naught out of heaven could be more grand. I have a book under my pillow, will one of you find it, for I am too weak to hold up my head?"

The book was found, and such a book. The leaves were made from a pennyworth of letter paper, the back was made from an old engine card, with the wire taken out, and inside was written in round hand, God's promises to orphan children. This singular treasure was all the property Philip had, and he gave it to one of the lads as a token of his love. Before we left, he requested we would sing " Hallelujah to the Lamb," and pray with him. We managed some way to sing, but when knelt round the bed, we remained silent from the depth of our emotion; Philip saw how we were affected, and placing his thin hands together, he said,—

"Oh, Jesus, Jesus, do bless us all, we shall never pray together again in this world; but do grant we may all meet in heaven; I am coming to Thee, and soon."

Philip could say no more, strength was gone; we all rose, and on leaving pressed his clammy fingers. His parting words were,

"I am a lonely lad, I have no relations or friends, will you come to my funeral, and carry me to my grave."

The Saturday following, we carried his cold remains, in a plain parish coffin, down the three flights of stairs, and laid it on a round, three-legged table, outside the house, and all with heads uncovered, standing round the coffin, sang,

"Oft as the bell with solemn toll."

We then silently bore the feeble frame of our young brother to the strangers' corner of St. Chad's cemetery (near the place where we afterwards laid the body of "Poor Joseph"), and saw the earth cover the body, but thought also of a soul, now glorified, and for ever with its Lord.

A BROKEN PROMISE.

THE wailing for two months for Jephthah's daughter on the mountains of Judea, because she was the victim of her father's thoughtless vow, and the last of his house, has taught many how necessary it is to be careful how we make a pledge. Hannah made a vow, and kept it. So did Jacob; he said, "If God will be with me, and keep me in this way that I go; and will give me bread to eat, and raiment to put on, so that I come to my father's house in peace; of all that thou shalt give me, I will surely give the tenth unto thee." It was the breaking of the last part of Jacob's vow that brought me a visitor from a distant town in July last. After introducing herself, the first question she asked was,—

"Do you believe in the unpardonable sin—the sin against the Holy Ghost? for I fear I have committed that sin, and the thought makes me very unhappy."

I

"I am glad to hear you say you are unhappy at the thought of having committed the unpardonable sin, for I think your sorrow on that account is an evidence you have not. Those who do sin that sin don't care, they are not at all concerned about it," I replied.

"Your answer gives me a little hope, but if I tell you more fully what I mean, you will be better able to advise with me.

"About three years since, in consequence of a special mercy, I made a vow to the Lord that as long as I lived I would dedicate a tithe or tenth part of all my income to His honour and for His glory. Give it to the church, the poor, the needy, the ministry, the missionary cause, and other objects which have for their purpose doing good. For several months I kept my word, but having got through my troubles, and a worldly spirit coming over me, I spent part of the money in useless things and needless dress, and took the other part to the bank. I was glad that I had told no one of my promise, so that I could not be charged with breaking it. But there was One who knew, and the inward witness which He has planted in every human heart has told me a thousand times of my broken vow; and the other day, I read

the fifth chapter of Acts, where Ananias and
Sapphira brought part of the money to Peter, yet
pretending to bring it all, and were struck dead
for their attempt at deception, their avarice having
prevailed over their honesty, for Satan filled their
hearts to lie and deceive, and they were frustrated.
I laid down the Bible, and became very miserable,
for I thought my case very like theirs. I, too,
had held back what had been vowed and conse-
crated to God, and from the same avaricious spirit;
they lied unto the Holy Ghost, and so have I.
What must I do ?"

"Are you a member of any Christian church ?"
I asked.

"Well, sir, I formerly took the sacrament; this
constitutes membership with us; but since I broke
my vow I have been afraid, and have sat at a distance to watch others, but durst not join them."

"Well, we know the Bible says, 'When thou
vowest a vow unto God, defer not to pay it: better
is it thou shouldest not vow, than that thou
shouldest vow and not pay.' Peter told Ananias
and Sapphira that while they had the land, or
after they had sold it, the property or money was
theirs; but having reckoned to give it all, and
keep part back, was the sin; and no doubt your

case is in a degree like theirs. It is a pity you broke your vow; it was a very good one, and it was easy to pay it."

"I now see and feel that I have done wrong, but I never was much of a giver. I have talked about a cheap religion, and thought anything given into the collecting box was lost, and might have been put to better use. I have proved the Scripture true, that 'he who soweth sparingly, shall reap also sparingly.' Several of my acquaintance have encouraged me in this worldly spirit, for they are often speaking against subscriptions, donations, and collections, saying that when people work for their money, they ought to please themselves what they do with it. I have been influenced by these arguments, and perhaps more by my own greedy propensities. I have subscribed to few charities, and this love of money has made my soul very lean."

"Yes, and it has made many souls lean besides yours. I know that greedy people are in the habit of saying, 'My power and the might of my hand hath gotten me this wealth,' forgetting that it is God that gives them power to get wealth more or less. I have recently seen in two Institutions several thousand persons, none of whom could earn their bread—some sick, some feeble, and some imbeciles; can these get riches? Health, strength, and reason are great blessings, and God gives them all."

"But do you not hear many complaints about having so many collections?" asked my visitor.

"Yes, but not from persons who give systematically," I replied. "These are the earnest workers in our chapels, and the salt of our churches. One of these told me, that when he was married he put a small book in his pocket, in which he entered all his givings. At the end of the year, and before he added it up, he guessed how much he had given, but found he had not given one half. He was much pained when he found out his mistake; and to avoid it in the future, adopted the giving a proportion. This man was like many others of God's humble servants, proved that 'it is more blessed to give than to receive.' People who are always crying out for a cheap religion should have what little they have very cheap, for they have very little. When we love God, we love to honour Him with all we are and all we have. The real Christian makes giving a means of grace, and when the church is right, all who go up to the temple to worship will go with an offering in their hand. The widow with her little copper mite, the mechanic with his silver, and the merchant with his gold,—all in proportion as God has blessed them. Begging sermons, bazaars, and begging letters will then be no more; the revenue of the church will be tenfold; and it will be more spiritual and prosperous. Some people talk and act as if their property was their own,— in a legal sense it may be, but not in the sight of God. He is the only proprietor; we are merely stewards. One of the dukes in the House of Lords said, 'Cannot I do what I will with mine own?' Why he had nothing; there is not a man in the world worth one penny. 'The earth is the Lord's, and the fulness thereof.' 'The silver is mine, and the gold is mine, saith the Lord of hosts.' The Crossley's, of Halifax, have wisely and thankfully inscribed over the almshouses they have built for the poor old people, 'Of thine own have we given thee.' If God gives me twenty shillings and I begrudge Him two, or one hundred pounds and I deny Him ten, it betrays a miserable soul. If we withold what we ought to give to good objects, it tendeth to poverty; but if we honour the Lord with our substance, and first part of our profits, with a single eye to His glory, He promises that our barns shall be filled with plenty, and when God promises, the thing promised is conveyed; He can fill them, and He will fill them. I know a poor, sick child of God whose great delight was to do all the good she could. Her income was five shillings per week, and out of that she gave five pence to missionary purposes, a benevolent society, and to others more needy than herself. A gentleman hearing of this sent her five pounds. She received it as from the Lord, saying, 'My dear Jesus has provided me with offerings for the next five years; the Lord will never be in debt to any of His creatures.'"

"My case looks worse and worse," said my visitor, "what must I do?"

"You must pay the money held back since you made your vow, with interest; pay it at once, will you?"

"Yes, I will, I feel in my soul I will, and thankful it is not too late. It shall be done the hour I return home. I know some poor objects it will do good. It shall be an offering to the Lord of His own," she replied.

"Well, then, you must get a small note-book, and write on the back, 'The Lord's Cash Book.'" Reckon what your income is from all quarters to the full, then put a tithe or tenth of that on the left hand side of the book, to be given to various purposes, as your judgment may determine. As you give, put that down on the right side, and add up from time to time to see if all be right."

"Would you advise me to confine myself to a tenth?"

"No, indeed. Give yourself fully to God, and then all other things will be easy. A tenth may do to begin with: give as the Lord prospers you. But I never knew any person who willingly, and from the heart, gave a tenth, who did not cheerfully and thankfully give more; and they all prove that "there is that scattereth and yet increaseth."

"I feel now the Lord will pardon me, and that I may go to the sacrament next month. I will watch and pray for strength to resist my avaricious propensity. Thank you, thank you for your advice."

My visitor left far more cheerful than she came, and I hope she will never again lose her peace of mind through breaking a good promise.

"LET ME PAT TURK."

WHEN Paul neared Damascus he was struck down by a dazzling light from heaven, and when able to speak, he said, "Lord, what wilt thou have me to do?" He was then told what his work was; and there is no doubt that all who are anxious to do good in God's own way, however humble, dangerous, or difficult the work, sinking their own will, and praying for the guidance of the Holy Spirit, are as verily directed into their own proper sphere as Paul was directed in his. The steps of a good man are ordered by the Lord as much now as ever, and He still directs their path; and there is no station, high or low, no condition or circumstance, in which we may not be useful. In some cases our usefulness may seem to be very little and feeble, but the future has often told a different tale. Here is one illustration.

I had been invited to a tea-meeting given by a benevolent gentleman to the blind. All the poor, dark creatures present were greatly elated with the treat. Some of them could sing, a few play on various instruments, others read a chapter from their Bible of raised letters, and several made speeches. One of the speakers, a thin, feeble creature, with a pale but beautiful countenance, and curly black hair, said,—

"Friends, I want to tell you something about a dog called Turk. One day I was thinking about my misfortune in being blind, and had become very sad and low in my mind. Oh! I thought, could I but work for my bread, and see the sun, the sky, the birds, the flowers, and especially the face of my mother, how happy I should be; and if I could see to read, I could teach the poor children in the ragged-school, and take good tracts to my neighbours, and so be useful to others. Well, a thought came, if I could get some tracts, and persuade some little girl to lead me, I would take them to the cottages. I prayed many times that the Lord would help me, and I told a good girl what I wanted. I asked her if she would take me to the tract depository. She very kindly did, and there I got a little basket full of tracts and small books; and on the Sunday afternoon, the good child led me amongst the houses to distribute them to the people who would have them. Most of them were kind to me, but one man was very cross, and the second Sunday he said,—

"'I thought I had ordered you not to come to this door with your rubbish.'

"'Yes, sir, you did.'

"'Then why do you come again?'

"'Well, sir, I have a fresh guide to-day, and she did not know of you refusing to have a tract; but you would please me much if you would have one this time, do please.'

"As I spoke, I held out my hand, containing a tract, touching the top of the chair on which he sat. The touch caused me to think he had taken it, and, letting go my hold, the tract fell to the floor. The white woolly dog instantly had the tract in his mouth, and squatting down on his hind legs, set bolt up, offering it to his master. The man's wife said,—

"'Now then, no one dare take that out of Turk's mouth but you, except they do not care for a bite, and you know the dog will sit there all day if you do not take it.'

"The man was now in a fix, and to please the dog took it out of his mouth, laying it on the mantelpiece, but determined not to read it. Being alone in the evening, and believing that no one could see him, he thought he would just see what the blind woman had brought. He took down the tract, and read it through, standing on the spot, for to his utter astonishment it was a correct description of himself, describing to the very life what he was, and clearly pointing out to him what he might be. It told of a man who for many years had lived a most wretched life,—drinking, swearing, card-playing, Sabbath-breaking, scoffing at the Bible and religion; a sullen, surly sinner, so miserable that life became a burden, and that he had made up his mind to drink himself to death. How, when going to the races, he saw on a barn door a placard with the words, 'The way of transgressors is hard,' and he thought if all the Bible be as true as that sentence, it is all true. The placard caused him to turn back. On his way home he met a boy, who gave him a tract, containing the first eighteen verses of the third chapter of Proverbs. He went early to bed, that he might read what the boy had given him unseen. Three days after, as the result of deep conviction for sin, earnest prayer, and believing on the Lord Jesus Christ, he became a changed and truly happy man, and, instead of drinking himself to death, joined the church, and lived to do much good.

"The man put the tract back on the mantelpiece, but still stood looking at it as it lay there. The first part of that man's history he knew was the history of himself; his wicked career had made his life a heavy burden, and he had often wished himself dead. He had intended to go to the public house that night as usual, but durst not; he suspected some one had given the blind woman the tract specially for him, and he had a very restless week. The Sunday morning following the dog began barking loudly at hearing a knock at the door; the man himself opened it, just in time to hear me say,—

"'Oh, this is the house where I must not leave any of my books; what shall I do?'

"'You must come in and sit down a moment, I want to ask you a few questions,' said the man.

"I entered the house with considerable fear, my guide leading me. The man took the tract out of his pocket, saying,—

"'Tell me who ordered you to leave this book here?'

"'No one ordered me, sir, for being blind I do not know the titles; I am told they are all good ones.'

"'I suspected some of my neighbours had. It seems very strange; I hope you will forgive my harsh conduct, and not pass the house without calling. I will pay you for this tract, for I must keep it.'

"When I heard this I called for the dog, for I remembered that it was he that had given the tract to his master, and I said,—

"'Let me pat Turk,' 'let me pat Turk; fine dog, Turk. He gave it to you, and you shall keep it.'

"He did keep it, and keeps it still, as a memorial of the mighty change wrought in his own soul,— a change from a sullen, surly sinner, to a cheerful, happy child of God."

Clapping of hands, and stamping of feet followed the blind girl's speech, and she sat down, having modestly and unconsciously taught us all a very useful lesson.

ROSE.

ALMOST every part of the old and new city of
Edinburgh may be seen from some of its
surrounding heights. Salisbury Crags, Arthur's
Seat, the Castle, and Calton Hill, all command an
extensive and interesting view of the hospitals,
schools, churches, halls, and squares. Scotchmen
may be pardoned for being rather proud of their
grand old Reekie, with its magnificent buildings,
and historic associations; for there is no doubt it
holds high its head amongst the capitals of Christ-
endom. But at the foot of Calton Hill there is
one huge edifice, with its massive iron gates se-
cured by ponderous locks and bars, which stands
as an evidence that schools and churches have not
yet done their work, and that the beautiful city
has at least one drawback. The builder of the
classic ruins which crown the summit of Calton
might probably call it "The Panopticon," but it

is better known by the toll-booth, or, better still, by jail or prison.

On my recent visit to Edinburgh, a note from the matron of this stronghold found its way to my temporary residence, urgently requesting me to conduct service in the female department. At the hour appointed, the bolts of the strong gates shot back for my admittance, not, I am thankfnl to say, as a prisoner, but going to tell my less favoured fellow-creatures of Him who preached deliverance to the captives, and shed His blood to set them free. The kind matron, Mrs. Aitken, was waiting my arrival, and conducted me to the strange " Assembly Hall," a large room lighted with a dome, and at one end, ranging one above the other, four crescent-shaped galleries, fronted with strong iron bars, forcibly suggesting a menagerie for wild beasts; and oh! melancholy truth, my audience consisted of one hundred and ten females, my own sisters, all peering through these firm fixed bars of iron. I have preached the Gospel in many strange places,—in taverns, barns, lodging-houses, factories, railway stations, theatres, circuses, reformatories, penitentiaries, and down coalpits,— but the scene then before me in Calton Bridewell leaves on my mind the strongest impression.

"Shall we open the service with singing?" I asked the matron.

"If you please, sir; they have all hymn books," was her reply.

I announced the hymn, but my heart was too full to look at my audience; and I knew what had made the difference betwixt the preacher and congregation. A full, soft voice, from about the centre of the lowest cell, raised the tune. It was one of those solemn, plaintive, Scotch airs that harmonise with the soul in sadness, and was much in keeping with the impressive words—"Behold the Saviour of mankind, nailed to the shameful tree." Most of the women sang, but many of them with faltering words and trembling voices. The words, the tune, the thoughts, calling back to memory other scenes and happier days, touched their hearts and affected their voices, and several were so overcome that they covered their faces and sat down ere the song was ended.

The subject of discourse was a scene once witnessed at Jerusalem, and related in the seventh chapter of Luke, when our Lord spoke words of comfort to a woman in deep sorrow. That woman's anguish of soul was such that she followed Jesus into the house of a man who regarded her

K

with the utmost abhorrence, who would have
spurned her from his door, and she knew it; but
so heavy was the load that crushed her agonised
soul that she could no longer bear it, she must tell
it to Jesus; and in despair she knelt at the feet of
Jesus, and bathed them with her tears. Speaking
of the scornful language of the haughty Pharisee,
when he said, "This man if he were a prophet,
would have known who and what manner of
woman this is that toucheth him, for she is a
sinner," we replied, He did know, He did know,
bless Him, He did know; and never did poor,
broken-hearted sinners come to Him yet but He
did know. He knows their deep contrition, knows
their distress, knows their unspeakable bitterness
of soul. He saw her heart was breaking, saw her
real grief, and knew it was for sin. She brought
her sins to Jesus, and in pity and tender compassion He said, "Thy sins are forgiven, thy faith hath
saved thee; go in peace." Merciful words; gracious
words. That moment He said "go in peace," He
gave her peace; and that moment was to that
woman a moment of boundless joy; her sins were
forgiven, God was reconciled. She entered the
Pharisee's house one of the most wretched women
in Jerusalem, yea in the world; she now leaves it

calm, peaceable, happy, indescribably happy.
Christ had saved her, and He receives all sinners
still.

Aprons, frocks, and handkerchiefs were in
general use behind the iron bars while this description of the tender compassion of our Lord to
the Jerusalem sinner was being given, for nothing
melts the heart like the love of Christ. There is
no love like His. There is no doubt that the most
of those one hundred and ten imprisoned creatures,
had by their conduct lost the love, friendship, or
regard of those who once cared for them; this
they knew, and it is a fearful thing to become an
outcast, forsaken by relations, frowned upon by
neighbours, and shunned by all. To know this,
must break the heart or make it like steel; lay us
in the dust, or rouse a spirit of stern defiance;
but to be told, to know, and better far to feel, that
there is One who still loves us; loves us though
we are cast off by all others; loves us in our
wretchedness and ruin, this blessed thought,
this sweet belief in this glorious truth, has healed
many a broken heart, and melted down the iron
and flinty soul.

Our concluding hymn contained the words—
"Jesus the name that charms our fears, that

bids our sorrows cease." The same voice again raised the tune, the solemn cadence reverberating round the dome, but not many sang. I and the matron assisted to swell the notes, because of the glorious words, for who would not sing of Him "who scatters all our guilty fears and turns our hell to heaven?" When the last note had died away, all heads were bowed to join in the benediction. A moment of silence followed and the service was over. Before parting, I requested the governess to introduce me to the young woman who so well conducted the singing. She instantly complied with my wish, and stepping to the front of the lower iron bars, by the moving of her finger brought the girl before us, but still behind the grating. She seemed to be about twenty-five years of age, pale, but rather good looking, she had an intelligent countenance, and under other influences, might very probably have been a great blessing to many. This nearer sight of her strengthened my desire to know a little more of her history, and I said, "My dear girl, I have been much pleased with your singing. I could not help thinking you have often sung in the sanctuary?"

"Yes, sir; many times."

"Did you ever attend the Sunday-school?"

" Yes, sir ; I went to Dr. Alexander's."

" How long did you go there ? "

" Until I was sixteen, sir."

" And what made you leave then, my child ? "

" I got fond of dress, mixed with gay companions, became idle, and took to drink and stealing."

" When does your term of imprisonment expire ? "

" I am transported for eight years, sir,"— weeping.

" Indeed, indeed ! Transported for eight years ! Poor, dear child ! Have you parents, or sisters, or brothers ? "

"Yes,"—still weeping,—" but my parents taught me no good ; they are both drunkards. One of my sisters is here, also transported."

" Had you remained in the Sunday-school, do you think you would have come here ? "

At this question she threw up both hands, fixed her eyes on the top of the grated cell, and with a voice of deep emotion exclaimed—

" Oh, no, sir ; no, sir. Sunday scholars never come here—never come here ; while they love the Sunday-school they will never come here. Oh ! that I had never left." That last sentence, " Oh ! that I had never left," was spoken with an emphasis, that told how deeply she regretted forsaking this guide of her youth, this influence for good; it was a false, fatal step, and she now bitterly deplored it.

I could endure no more. I put my hand through the bars—she held it long in both of hers—and bidding her and her hundred and nine companions in bonds farewell, left the sad scene behind; but have many times thought of that memorable day, and often, in hours of stillness and quietness, when the mind was reviewing the scenes of the past, have I heard from behind those bars the plaintive strains of poor, transported ROSE ANNA.

MY FIRST BOOK.

HOW I learned to read I can scarcely tell. As far back as memory will go a juvenile friend lent me a little halfpenny book, called the " Babes in the Wood," with a rude picture of two children lying dead under a tree, and the Robin Redbreasts bringing leaves to cover them. The sorrowful story roused all my young emotion, and I have had considerable respect for the petulant, unsocial Robin ever since. I have often watched him, especially in the Autumn evenings, standing on the topmost twig of our dark leaved holly, singing his sweet sad song; might it not have been his funeral dirge over the hapless babes? The same young friend brought me another halfpenny volume, also with pictures, containing an account of the tragic end of poor Cock Robin, and a third about the sickness of Jenny Wren; and for months after I was greatly puzzled with the doctor's opinion about the cause of Jenny Wren's dying. The sage physician said,—

> "The cause of her death
> Was the want of more breath."

It seemed strange to me that Jenny did not breathe, and save her own life. These tiny volumes of fiction leave an indelible impression on the minds of young readers, teaching us all how important it is, that little folks should have true and good little books.

What influence these three deeply interesting narratives had in giving me a love for reading, or creating a desire for other books, I cannot tell; but I do know that I had an intense wish to have a library of my own, but circumstances were greatly against me, so I was content and glad to borrow where I could, and when I could. A little, stout, red-faced man, called Westall, who wore a broad-brimmed hat, and kept a second-hand bookstall in our market, a mighty man in my estimation, was very kind to me. No doubt he suspected the state of my pockets, but in his good nature he allowed me to stand at one end of his stall where I should be out of the way of his richer customers, and in the corner I read the wonderful volumes, with such deep enjoyment and delight, that I frequently

forgot time or weather, and many times when the
hour came for moving off I had lost the use of my
feet, or felt as if I was without toes. There was
one book that greatly astonished me, it was the
first geography I had ever seen. On the first page
there was a small round card like a clock face,
held in the middle with a piece of thread; on
turning it round it showed in what part of the
world it was light, and where it was dark; on
another page there was a view of the northern
regions, with their icebergs, snow mountains,
white bears, and diminutive Esquimaux; on
another the naked, dark aborigines of Australia
with their boomerangs, and a North American Indian
with his tomahawk; on another the African Negro
in his chains; on another Lions, Tigers, and other
wild beasts roaming through the jungles of India;
and last a map of the world, with its north and
south poles, its torrid, temperate, and frigid zones.
I read much of this remarkable book standing in
my corner, and would have given all my property
to have called it my own. It greatly expanded
my view of the world, for up to that time I was
something like J. Midgley, a respectable old
weaver, who resided on the top of our Yorkshire-
street, whom a few friends induced to accompany

them to a neighbouring mount called Brown
Wardle; he was sixty years of age, but had never
been many yards from home before; on reaching
the top of the hill, he looked round with amaze-
ment, exclaiming "I didn't think England had
been so big." My knowledge of Geography was
much like Midgley's. An old family Bible, with
many wonderful illustrations, was often my companion. The pictures in that book, and especially
the pictures of Joseph being sold for a slave, and
then being raised next to the king; of Samson
slaying the lion, and pulling down the temple of
Dagon; of little David with his sling meeting
Goliath; and of Elijah being fed by the ravens;
of the angels singing at Bethlehem; of our Saviour
ascending into heaven; and of the last judgment;—
all these are still visible to my mental vision, and
no doubt have had an influence over me for good,
for I still remember how deeply I was interested
in all these events.

Good natured Mr. Westall not only allowed me
to stand in the corner and read for nothing, but
lent me several small books of travel, and a
Pleasing Instructor. One Saturday evening he
sold Plutarch's Lives, in six volumes; when he
had tied them up, and the man had paid down the

price, he said to the purchaser, "That lad in the corner envies you of your bundle, he will miss those books."

The man looking at me replied, "Well, my lad, if you will come to my house, I will lend you the first volume, after I have read it, but you must keep it clean and not turn down the leaves;" he then told me where he resided, and promised the book in a fortnight.

I was at his house, three miles away, at the time fixed, and returned with such a treasure as none but a bookworm can conceive. For several months I was living with Theseus, Romulus, Solon, Pericles, Lycurgus, and other mighty heroes of past ages; moving amidst scenes and events that had transpired thousands of years before I was born: the rise and fall of kings and kingdoms, the deeds of fleets and armies; the sayings and doings of sages and statesmen, all rose up before me as I turned over page after page, and my life in a few months seemed to expand into centuries. My ambition was now roused, and I longed to be able to visit those classic lands, and tell something more about their marvellous history; and amongst my many blessings I count it no small one that I have since been able to accomplish this intense desire.

But strong as was my love for books, I could find no pleasure in mere novels. These fumes of wild, foolish fancy, these inventions of perverted souls and sickly brains, feeding and pandering to the simple, the silly, and the sensual, were to me always repulsive. This class of novels may vary in name and scenery, but they have the same old, seedy, worn-out dolls to exhibit, always—

> Loving and loathing, eloping, relenting,
> Slaying and stealing, rejoicing, repenting,
> Intriguing, lusting, and lying,
> Pouting and fainting, laughing and flirting,
> Deceiving, believing, insulting, deserting,
> Weeping, sighing, and dying.

Heart and intellect must both wither under the pernicious influence of these impure associations. They are a moral pestilence; they take away the power or wish to read more solid, profitable, and useful books. I know there is a difference in novels, but the most popular and extensive novel writer of this age has not one sentence in all his works that could show a weary soul the way to rest. Novels utterly unfit us for real, true, earnest life. A woman, who her husband said had the misfortune to be married, could tell the names of all the new novels, but not the name of one joint of meat, or of few books in the Bible.

After finishing Plutarch's Lives, for I borrowed all the six volumes, "Young's Night Thoughts" next engrossed my attention. This work was a treasure indeed, leading me out into higher and sublimer regions of thought. These first lines I read in Young follow me to this hour:—

> "Faith builds a bridge from this world to the next,
> O'er death's dark gulf, and all its horror hides;
> Prayer ardent opens heaven, lets down a stream
> Of glory on the consecrated hour
> Of man, in audience with the Deity."

These books gave me an ardent desire to know more. Oh! how I yearned to go to some good school where I could have a better education. I was a few months at the National School, Red Cross Street, at the time Mr. Davenport was the master, and well remember old Mr. James Royds. and Mr. R. Elliott giving us all a new shilling and a medal on the day George the Fourth was crowned. We were ordered to hang the medals on our buttons, and attend St. Mary's Chapel on the following Sunday. But I had soon to leave this seminary to earn my bread. I loved the Sunday-school, and there, like many more poor children,. got most of my education. My ignorance of the. meaning of words greatly perplexed me in all my reading, for my vocabulary was very contracted; I don't remember having then seen or heard of a dictionary, but a little incident led to my obtaining the great prize. I had a young companion who attended High Street Chapel, and sometimes I went with him on the Sunday evening. At that time the Choir at this place of worship had obtained great renown, and I, amongst others, went to hear them sing. They were led by Mr. John Butterworth, who took considerable pains to train his band of singers; the organist was Mr. John Roby, of the firm of Fenton and Roby, Bankers, and the author of the Traditions of Lancashire. The Minister of High Street Church, Mr. John Ely, was an accomplished scholar, and a very popular preacher, but his language was far above my comprehension. I well remember that one evening when wedged in a corner of a little pew in the extreme part of the gallery, Mr. Ely in his sermon frequently mentioned the word "Prerogative;" why this word should hold so fast to me I cannot tell, but in my walk home I over and over again found myself saying, Prerogative, Prerogative. On the Monday morning I went to a man whom I thought the wisest in our locality, and said,—

"Adam, can you tell me the meaning of the word Prerogative?"

"No, I cannot, and there is no one in this neighbourhood can; where has thou heard that word?"

"Mr. Ely often used the word in his sermon, last night," I replied.

"Well, then, go and ask him the meaning, for no one here knows."

"Is there a book that tells the meaning of such words?" I again asked.

"Yes, Johnson's Dictionary, but I don't know where there is one. Thy father is taking in Buchan's Domestic Medicine in numbers, when the number man calls, ask him about the Dictionary."

I was impatient to see the "Number Man," so called from supplying his customers with parts of the book, from part first or number one, up to the end of the work. At last the august personage came, laid number nine on the table and got his sixpence. To this hour the appearance of that important man is imprinted on my memory. He was a stout, brown-faced, broad-faced man, with a glazed hat, dark green coat with metal buttons, a black bag, and a thick stick to hook his bag upon; he travelled for a Mr. Harrison. I watched him wrap up his grand books and walk away without saying a word to him about the Dictionary, for having no money, I was afraid to speak to him, but I followed after him for about a hundred yards, and then called out,—

"I say."

He turned quickly round, and looking right at me, replied,

"What do you say ?"

He knocked all my say out of me; he saw he had done so, and laughing, he gently asked,

"What do you say, my boy ? "

"Is there a book that tells the meaning of Prerogative and other words ? "

"Yes, my child, there is Johnson's Dictionary, do you want one ? "

"Yes, sir, how much will it cost ? "

"Two and sixpence; if I bring you one the next time I come, how much can you pay me per month ? "

This question was a serious one, and how to answer it was the difficulty, at last I replied,

"Twopence."

He burst out into loud laughter, at my simplicity, but his good nature prevailed, and to my intense joy he told me he would bring me a Dictionary the next month, and still laughing said,—

"You must get your twopence ready, my boy."

The next question was, how must I raise the twopence, for if a man has not twopence he has not twopence, and this was just my condition, and my poor, dear mother had not one halfpenny to spare, and I could not ask her for anything. There was an aged man residing in a cellar near our house whom we called old James; he was a weaver of woollen, and had the looms in his house. He one day had a load of coals pushed down at his door; the moment I saw these coals it struck me I might earn a penny. So I went for our shovel and broom, took up the little door that covered the coal-house, and without being requested or asking permission, began to tumble the coal down the hole. Hard I worked, and hard did I sweat, gathering up every portion, and then sweeping all up quite clean, all the time looking out at the corner of my eyes for the old man to come out, to praise me, and give me something, but he not coming I ventured down the four steps, opened the door a few inches, timidly saying,

"Old James."

"What?"

L

" I have got your coals in."

" Very well."

I quietly closed the door, walked up the steps very down-hearted, but saying to myself, Is that all ? After pondering the matter over a few minutes, I again got the broom and again swept about making all cleaner still, and again ventured down the steps, and opening the door about two inches again said,

" Old James."

" What ? "

" I have got your coals in."

"And I will coals thee if thou comes here again, who told thee to touch the coals ? "

As he said the last words he threw a handful of empty bobbins rattling against the door, which made me scamper up the steps again pretty quickly, but was not I wrath ! My indignation was awful, if it had mattered anything ; I could have taken the coals out of the hole again, and scattered them all over the district. I expected at least a penny, but, ah me, all was over, and all this puffing and sweating for nothing, and bobbins thrown after me in the bargain.

What next. Well the next was, that I went to offer my services to a neighbouring woman whose husband worked about two miles distant, and sometimes she had to seek amongst us little folks to get some one to take his dinner, so to secure this job entirely to myself, I offered to take the dinner for a halfpenny per time, and she very willingly made the contract.

So I walked with the man's dinner two miles there, and had to return two miles back; four times four, sixteen miles for my first twopence towards buying my first book.

What a struggle, but what a victory; for I was now prepared for the great bookseller, the important "Number Man," and almost counting the hours when he would come.

Thank God for books, and especially good books. They are the spirits of the noble and mighty in all ages, revealing to us their best thoughts, speaking to us in their best language, condescending to visit alike the king on his throne, the peasant in his cot, the shepherd in his hut, or the philosopher in his study; they unrol to us the records of ancient days, bringing remote events to present view, they draw aside for us the curtain of the heavens, show us the wonders of the earth, and uncover the depths of the seas. They take us into their utmost confidence, tell us of their joys and sorrows, introduce us to their choicest friends, and sing for us their sweetest songs; they retire at our bidding, come again at our request, and of doing all they can to instruct and please us, they are never, never weary.

My twopence was now ready, and I was anxiously looking out for the "Number Man." At last he came, and how my heart did beat as he opened his black bag and brought out my new Dictionary, I gave him my *warm* twopence, he took the money and again laughed at me; I could now join in the laugh for I had got my first own book, my long coveted treasure. It was soon backed with blue-glazed calico to keep it clean, and my name written in large hand on the back that all might see to whom it belonged. Dr. Johnson was now my learned tutor, and for years I never read a book without having him by my side. He told me not only the meaning of Prerogative, but hundreds of other words that my neighbour Adam did not know. There are many volumes around me in the little room where I am writing this short sketch, some large and costly, others small but valuable, but none have been obtained with the same depth of feeling I had when paying down my twopence and securing My First Book.

THE CONTEST.

IN a little chamber, connected with the hair-dressing shop of Mr. John Pollitt, in the old market place, Rochdale, sat nine men, all thoughtful and serious, and sometimes all silent; for the subject before them was of a character that required careful consideration, and they were afraid of taking an injudicious step, lest they should increase the evil they were anxious to remove. These nine men were the committee of the Sunday School Union, and the absorbing question before them was the coming Rochdale races. The injury done to the youths of the various schools by the previous races had been so evident, and had so distressed their teachers that they looked forward with perfect dread to the consequences of those approaching; and what to do in order to counteract their pernicious influence was the perplexing thought.

The scenes witnessed at any of these gatherings of the vast multitude, viewed from a moral point, are very deplorable; publicans erecting their forests of booths and tents for selling their fiery, maddening liquors; the reckless, the profligate, and the idle gathered from surrounding towns and neighbouring counties; dens of thieves and houses of infamy pouring out their contents to ply their trade; pickpockets and professional gamblers, blacklegs, and turf-men holding high revel; mills standing, factories closed, husbandry and trade suspended; the thoughtless, the foolish, the inexperienced, the heartless knave and hardened villain mingling and crowding from east, west, north, and south,—from highways, byways, hills and valleys, all converging towards one fatal centre, and constituting a real pandemonium, while the yells of the victors, the imprecations of the vanquished, the oaths and curses of the drunkard make the whole scene truly awful. And when the races are over, when this tide of increased wickedness and multiplied iniquity rolls back,—every soul is deeper stained in sin, and sunk to a lower state of moral degradation. And all this to see brutes, less brutish than their owners, and far less than many of the spectators, goaded on by shouts, the cutting lash, and cruel spur, to run beyond their natural strength.

Was it a wonder, then, that good men,—those

lovers of God and man, whom God calls the salt of the earth and the light of the world, who sigh and cry for the abominations that be done,—was it surprising that they should feel sad and concerned at the prospective havoc which was coming to their neighbours, and the young of their churches and schools? One of the nine teachers suggested that bills and placards, with passages of Scripture in large letters, should be posted on trees, walls, gables, fences and gates, observing that the hardened in rebellion might probably deride, scorn, and laugh at them, but that those whose hearts were yet soft, and whose consciences were not yet seared, might be influenced by them, and possibly be saved. Another recommended tea meetings at the various schools to keep them at home. Another thought that taking them out of the town on excursion trips would put them out of danger. And a fourth recommended a general prayer meeting of all the teachers, to implore heaven's protecting care over the young of the various schools, and that we should send two well-known labourers in the Sunday School to the men constituting the committee of management for the races, and implore them for their own sake, and for the sake of troubled fathers and mothers, and especially for the sake of the

youth of the town and neighbourhood to give the
races up.   There was no objection to placards, none
to tea meetings, none to excursions, none to a
general prayer meeting; but to induce the mana-
gers and promoters of the races to abolish them
altogether seemed out of the question.   But one
more daring than the rest, nominated two friends
and workers in the church and Sunday school, and
obtained a pressing and unanimous request that
they would undertake the cause of the imperilled
young, and if possible persuade the racing gentlemen to abandon their degrading sports ; and before
the nine men separated, prayer, earnest and fervent
prayer was offered on their behalf, that God would
make their way prosperous.

By communicating with the racing secretary, it
was ascertained when the ringleaders and cham-
pions in the wholesale abominations would
meet; the day and hour came, and they were
assembled in the large chamber of the Woolpack
Inn, but from some cause only one of the delegates
made his appearance.   He ascended the stairs,
knocked at the door, and presented to one of the
gentlemen a letter addressed to the chairman, containing a copy of the resolution of the committee
of the Sunday School Union, with a very respect-

ful request for an interview, and then retired to a small side room, waiting for a reply, and pleading with heaven for success. He had to wait a considerable time, for the teachers' request had rather embarassed the racing fraternity, but an interview was granted. The chairman sat at the head of a long table, and the gentlemen, many of them publicans, composing the committee, down each side.

The one delegate, the single Sunday School teacher, took his appointed place at the opposite end of the table. After a pause the president said,—

"You are the bearer of a resolution from the committee of the Sunday School Union of this town requesting us not to go on with the races, and also a request for an interview; would you briefly state your object in seeking the interview?"

The teacher replied,—

"Well, gentlemen, I am truly obliged for your kindness in receiving our resolution, and your courtesy in allowing me to urge its request. I am known to you all, and you are all known to me. Many of you are parents, and dearly love your children, and it would be to you a great trouble to see any of them fall victims to evil influences. You would rather see them die in their innocence and be taken to heaven in their infancy. Thousands of fathers and mothers in the town and neighbourhood have the same feelings with regard to their children, and they have the greatest dread of your coming races; and the feeling of love and fear for the young is shared by hundreds of Sunday School teachers, and many of them have not ceased to pray night and day that the lambs of their flock might be saved this impending evil; for to many the Sunday before the races will be their last Sabbath in the School. I know some of the teachers have earnestly besought the Almighty that He would change your hearts, and incline you to listen to the respectful and earnest request now made; and I am sure I join them. It would be one of those deeds you would look back upon with satisfaction, and for which you would receive my thanks, and blessings from trembling, godly men."

A pause followed, then a few whispers at the head of the table, then a request that the teacher would retire for a few moments. He again stepped into the little side room, and again prayed to God for success, and was again summoned into the large room to hear the verdict. The chairman said,—

"We have carefully, and we think fairly, considered your very respectful address, but find that we are too far gone to acceed to your wish; several stands and huts are already let; and besides, we have a debt of near one hundred pounds, which we must pay, that is our principal difficulty."

The teacher replied,—

"I am very sorry, gentlemen, to hear your decision, and the committee and teachers will be greatly dejected when I give my report. But if the debt be your strongest reason for having the races, I will pay the debt any day you like."

"You pay the debt, pay it out of your own pocket?" asked the chairman in astonishment.

"Not out of my own pocket, gentlemen; I shall only need to tell the teachers and scholars, and the money will be subscribed in one week, perhaps in one day."

This offer took them all by surprise, and the way the money would be raised took evident effect. They saw it would be done. There was no doubt about it.

Whispers were again exchanged, and the delegate was again requested to retire a moment, and again he entered the little side room, and again breathed his prayer to God. In about twenty minutes the door was opened; all the gentlemen stood on their feet and seemed considerably excited, and the answer this time was,—

"We have again considered your request, and your spirited offer to meet all our liabilities, but the matter is too far gone; we think we are bound to have the races this year; but we pledge our word that, as far as our influence goes, these will be the last Rochdale races."

It is now upwards of twenty years since this anxious and exciting interview took place, and to whatever influence it may be attributed, there have been no Rochdale races since. We think that prayers were heard; that the force of the request was felt; that the hearts of the men were softened, and better thoughts prevailed. Let God be praised, and He only have all the glory. Does He not say, "If ye abide in me, and my words abide in you, *ye shall ask what ye will*, and it shall be done unto you"?

Tubbs and Brook, Printers, Manchester.

LIST OF WORKS

PUBLISHED BY

TUBBS & BROOK,

11, MARKET STREET, MANCHESTER.

Should there be any difficulty in obtaining from the local Bookseller, T. & B. will forward any of the Books above 5d. post free for Published Price in Stamps.

SIMPLE RECORDS.

BY JOHN ASHWORTH,

AUTHOR OF "STRANGE TALES."

Cloth, 1/6. In Packets, on thin paper, 9d.

CONTENTS.

Little Sandy	Kate
New Eyes	Willy
The Three Sisters	Lucy Smith
The New Mound	A Mistake
A Troublesome Halfpenny	Old Thomas
The Three Truant Boys	Rachel Riley
The New Shawl	Philip
I'm too Big Now	A Broken Promise
Where's my Jacket?	"Let me pat Turk"
Shall we Expel Him?	Rose
The Brothers	My First Book
Edward's Grave	The Contest
The White Frock	

Queen's Edition of Strange Tales.
 Illustrated, beautifully bound, gilt edges, 9/-.

Large Type Edition.
 Illustrated, plain edges, 6/6.

 ⁎⁎ For other Editions see next page.

WALKS IN CANAAN.

By same Author. 304 pages, with 7 full-page illustrations: Cloth 2/6 ; extra cloth. gilt edges, 3/6.

STRANGE TALES FROM HUMBLE LIFE,
BY JOHN ASHWORTH.

Fine Edition, Four Series, cloth limp, 1/6 each. The First and Second, bound in one volume, cloth, boards, 3/0; or, extra cloth, gilt edges, with steel portrait of the Author, 4/0; also Third and Fourth in one volume, 3/0; gilt edges, 4/0.

These remarkable Tales are still kept as Tracts, at 1d. each, of which nearly Three Millions have already been sold.

First Series.

1. Mary : a Tale of Sorrow.
2. The Dark Hour. [Men.
3. A Wonder ; or The Two Old
4. Sanderson and Little Alice.
5. Wilkins. [and II.
6. & 7. The Dark Night. Parts I.
8. Joseph : or, The Silent Corner.
9. My Mother.
10. Niff and his Dogs.
11. My New Friends. Part I.
12. My New Friends. Part II.
13. My New Friends. Part III.

Second Series.

14. Mothers. [Prayer.
15. Twenty Pounds ; or The Little
16. All is Well.
17. My Uncle; or, Johnny's Box.
18. Old Adam.
19. Ellen Williams.
20. Trials.
21. Answered at Last.
22. Priscilla. [Step.
23. Julia ; or, The First Wrong
24. No Cotton.
25. My Young Ragged Friends.

Third Series.

26. The Lost Curl.
27. Emmott.
28. The Widow.
29. Sarah ; or, "I will have Him!"
30. My Sick Friends. Part I.
31. My Sick Friends. Part II.
32. George.
33. James Burrows.
34. John and Mary.
35. A Sad Story.
36. Lucy's Legacy.
37. Edmund.

Fourth Series.

38. The Golden Wedding.
39. William the Tutor.
40. Fathers.
41. Little Susan.
42. Old Matthew.
43. Old Ab'.
44. Milly.
45. The Fog Bell.
46. Mrs. Bowden.
47. Happy Ned.
48. Harry.
49. A Dancer.

Fifth Series.

50. The Old Deacon.
51. The Red Lamp.
52. Billy Bray.

.*. "Mr. Ashworth's Tales and Books are above my praise; they are circulated, I believe, not by thousands, but by millions, and the result is the name of John Ashworth is a Household Word, not only in the halls, but in the lowly homes of England."—*Dr. Guthrie.*

Lancashire: its Puritanism and Nonconformity.

By Robert Halley, D.D. In 2 vols., demy 8vo., with maps and plates, price 30/-.

A Cheap Edition, in 1 vol., will shortly be published. Price 7/6.

"A great story told very well, in a fair spirit, and a readable style."—*Athenæum.*

"An elaborate and thoughtful work. * * * The events are related by Dr. Halley with ability, knowledge, and fairness: and his book is eminently deserving of attention."—*Daily News.*

"Dr. Halley's work is not merely a local history, though this is all it professes to be. It is that and something more."—*British Quarterly Review.*

David Lloyd's Last Will.

By Hesba Stretton. 6/-.

Lectures to Children.

By the Rev. John Crawshaw. Fcap. 8vo., Tenth Thousand. Cloth, 1/0; gilt edges, 1/6.

"It is a gem."—*Wesleyan Magazine.*

"The subjects are treated in a most interesting and fascinating manner."—*Baptist Reporter.*

"We can heartily recommend this little work."—*Christian Spectator.*

"This little book is full of instruction for mothers and children, written in a popular style."—*Mothers' Friend.*

"High and holy lessons of Divine truth in the most simple language; aided by singularly apt illustrations."—*Portsmouth Guardian.*

Also by the same Author.

Fireside Conversations about Wesley.

Fcap. 8vo., Second Edition. Cloth, 1/0; gilt, 1/6.

Facts about Boys.

Fcap. 8vo., Second Edition. Cloth, 1/6; gilt, 2/0.

Tales from Manchester Life.

By a Manchester Minister. Price 1d. each.

No. 1—Annie, the Maid of the Mill | No. 3—Uncle Bob
„ 2—Our Tom | „ 4—A Tale for Christmas.

Joe and the Squire.

A Blind Minister's Story. Price 1d.

Alpha; or God in Matter. Cloth, 4/-.

British War History during the Present Century.

By William Stokes. 2/6.

Tender Herbs; or, Lessons for the Lambs.

By Rev. G. W. Conder. 12 Nos. at 2d.; or bound in cloth, with Illustrations, 2/6; extra cloth gilt, 3/6.

Life Scenes : By William Walker.
No. 1.—Olive's Danger. | No 2.—Under the Ice.
Price 1d. each. Others in preparation.

Victory and Service.
Illustrated by Sermons on the Book of Joshua. By Rev. C. D. Marston. M.A., Rector of Kersal, Manchester. Crown 8vo., price 6/0.

Six Sermons.
In paper cover. By Rev. C. D. Marston. Price 6d.

Queen of Beauty for the Throne of Fashion.
Crown 8vo., price 6d.

True Tales from Common Life.
The Young Sinner and the Old Saint. Price 1d.

Bishop Latimer's Sermon on the Plough.
Fcap. 8vo., 40 pages, price 1d.

Ecumenical Councils, Six Lectures on
By William Urwick, M.A., Minister of Hatherlow Chapel. Crown 8vo., cloth, lettered, 2/0.

Sunday Thoughts ;
Or, Great Truths in Plain Words. By Mrs. T. Geldart. Sixth edition—16th thousand. Cloth, 2/6 ; cloth, extra gilt sides and edges, 3/0.
This Work is designed for Young People, from five to fifteen, and contains numerous illustrative explanations of Scripture. It will be found a valuable and handsome gift book for the young of either sex.

Memorials of Rev. William J. Shrewsbury.
By his Son, John V. B. Shrewsbury. Fourth Edition. Price 5/0, with portrait.

Finney's (Rev. C. G.) Sermons.
Preached in Manchester, 1860. 162 pages, 1/0.

The Four Evangelists.
Their distinctive designs and peculiarities.—A most valuable book for Sunday School Teachers, and others engaged in the study of the Gospels. Paper cover, 6d.

Bible Lessons for the Infant Class and Nursery.
200 pages, cloth lettered, price 1/6.

Little While, and other Poems.
By Mrs. Crewdson. Third Edition, on fine toned paper, elegantly bound in cloth, gilt edges, 2/6 ; extra gilt, 3/6.
May also be had as Leaflets, in packets of 100, 1s.

Aunt Jane's Verses.
By the same Author, Illustrated edition, gilt edges, 3/6.

Tales and Sketches.

By Rev. J. M. Russell.

	Without Cover.	With Cover.
The Merchant-Missionary - - - - -	2d.	3d.
The Cant of Science - - - -	2d.	3d.
Lottie Selkirk : A Tale for the Young - -		6d.
The Light of Common Life - - - -		9d.

The above bound in cloth, 2s. 6d.

OPINIONS OF THE PRESS.

"These *Tales* are written from a Christian, and some of them from a Temperance, point of view, and are intended to convey principles belonging to both. There is some smartness in the telling of the stories. They are evidently meant to be read, and they will be read with avidity by the *people*—for whom, we presume, they have been written by one of themselves."—*Literary World.*

"Your book shows real feeling and real ability: it has piety and humanity."—*Rev. T. T. Lynch.*

"The Sketches are written in a style particularly adapted to the young, by whom they will be read with especial interest."—*Liverpool Mercury.*

"A work we can commend to the notice of our readers. The 'Light of Common Life' is a tale we especially admire,—it is natural, simple, and interesting."—*Onward.*

"We think Mr. Russell lays us under obligation for the rebukes which, in the shape of short and very readable tales, he administers to certain notions which we cannot but think are sadly too prevalent in the present day."—*Bury Visitor.*

Stowell's (The late Canon) Pleasures of Religion.

And other Poems. Cloth gilt, 1/6.

The Christian Sabbath.

Its Claims, Duties, and Privileges. By W. H. Llewellyn. Paper cover, 4d.

Form of Freedom.

Five Colloquies on Liturgies. By Rev. S. Clarkson. 1/0.

The Church at Home.

A Plea for Family Religion. By Rev. S. Clarkson. 1/0.

The Divine Idea of the Church.

A Sermon to Young Men. By Rev. H. Batchelor. 6d.

Ought Bishops to have Seats in Parliament ?

The Debate in the House of Commons, 1837. Re-published By G. Hadfield, Esq., M.P. Price 6d.

The Eastern Question ; or, War and Prophecy.

Crown 8vo., 32 pages. 2d.

Ready Reckoner. 32mo., 192 pages. 6d.

Woman and the Times we Live In.
> By Mrs. S. A. Sewell. Crown 8vo., printed cloth covers, 1/- ; cloth, lettered, 1/6 ; cloth, gilt edges, 2/-.

Folk Song and Folk Speech of Lancashire.
> On the Ballads and Songs of the County Palatine. By W. E. A. Axon, F.R.S.L. Cloth, 1/6 ; paper cover, 1/0.

India and Palestine;
> Or, the Restoration of the Jews. By Thomas Clarke. Paper cover, 3d.

The Name of God in 405 Languages.
> Paper cover. Price 2d.

Origin of the World, and the Mosaic Creation;
> Or, Genesis and Geology. By John Cobley. Price 1/0.

The Great Snobocracy;
> Or, Men and Women of the Time. Price 1d.

Eight Christmas Carols. Music and Words, 1d.

Anniversary Music.
> For Sunday School Festivals. Nine pieces, 1d.

Select Missionary Pieces.
> Ten pieces in Four parts. Words in full. Sewed, 1d.

Select Songs and Anthems.
> Six pieces in Four parts. Words in full. Sewed, 1d.

Map of Manchester.
> Divided into Sections, with List of, and References to, the Streets, &c. Neatly done up for the pocket, 6d.

Factory Books and Forms.
> Published by authority of Her Majesty's Inspector.

The Physician's Daughter.
> A Tale founded on Facts. 2d.

The Upstarts.
> A Comedy in Four Acts. Price 1/0.

Readings selected from Mursell's Lectures. Cloth, 1/0.

Levers to Lift the Lowly.
> Lecture by Rev. A. Mursell. Price 1d.

Fireside Pictures.
> By Rev. A. Mursell. Crown 8vo., illustrated. Price 3d.

Past Labours in Sunday Schools.
> By J. Walker. Price 1/6.

TEMPERANCE PUBLICATIONS.

" Prepare ye the Way of the Lord."
> A Sermon preached by the Rev. Chas. Garrett, in Spurgeon's
> Tabernacle, on behalf of the National Temperance League.
> 35th thousand.   Price 1d.

Stop the Gap !   A Plea for Bands of Hope.
> By the Rev. Chas. Garrett.   Price 1d.

" Drinking Himself Drunk."
> An Old Story with a Modern Application.   By Rev. E.
> Hewlett.   Price 1d.

Prohibition Movement in the New England States.
> By Hon. G. H. Vibbert.   Price 1d.

Is Alcohol a Necessary of Life ?
> By Dr. H. Munro.   1d.

A Plea for Total Abstinence.
> By Rev. A. Clarke.   Price 1d., or 5/0 per 100.

Beardsall's Temperance Hymn Book,
> Contains 270 Hymns suitable for Public and Social Temper-
> ance Meetings.   55th thousand.   Cloth limp, 6d. ; cloth
> boards, 8d. ; roan, 10d.

Ditto.   Large type, cloth, 1/0 ; roan, 1/6.

Band of Hope Treasury,
> Contains Music (both Notations), Dialogues, Recitations,
> and Sketches.
>> First Series, 64 pages, 6d.
>> Second Series, 148 pages, 9d.
>> First and Second Series, cloth, 1/6.
>> New Series, 1870, 120 pages, 1/4, 9d., and 6d.
>>> Ditto,   1871,   do.   do.   do.   do.
>>> *** Published Monthly, price ½d.

Temperance Pledge Book,
> Neatly done up for the pocket.   Prices : 32 leaves, 6d. ;
> 80 leaves, 1/0.

Hoyle's Popular Band of Hope Melodist,
> Containing 160 Hymns.   Paper, 1d ; cloth, 2d.

Hoyle's Hymns and Songs
> For Temperance Societies and Bands of Hope.   1½d.
> Ditto, large paper edition.   Cloth, 4d.

Hoyle's Music Book for Hymns and Songs.
> Old Notation, paper cover, 1/4 ; cloth, 2/0.
> New Notation,   „   8d. ;   „   1/0.

Hoyle's Reciter.
> 54 Recitations and Dialogues.   1d.

SUNDAY SCHOOL HYMN AND TUNE BOOKS.

Popular Sacred Harmonies,

    For Home and Sunday School. 220 pieces in three parts, with Words—Arranged for the Voice or the Pianoforte. By the Rev. John Compston. Cloth, 1/6; cloth, gilt, 2/0. Ninth edition—23,000.

Ditto, with Supplement, cloth, red edges, 2/0.

Ditto, Tonic Sol-fa Notation. This Edition contains 253 pieces in four parts, with Words underlined, and *an entire Hymn* for each Tune—making it complete in itself as a HYMN AND TUNE BOOK. Extra cloth, limp, red edges, 2/0.

Supplement to Sacred Harmonies,

    Established Notation. Containing Christmas Carols, Anniversary Pieces, Missionary Pieces, and Select Songs and Anthems, in all 33 pieces in four parts, with the entire Words. Neat paper cover, 6d.

Sacred Songs for Home and School.

    New and enlarged edition, containing 328 selected Hymns, suitable for Sunday Schools, Families, and Meetings. 400th thousand. *This is the most complete Selection of its kind,* containing nearly all the pieces generally used in Sunday Schools. They are arranged under different subjects, with Index of first lines, and references to suitable Tunes in POPULAR SACRED HARMONIES. In paper, 2d.; cloth, 3d.; roan, 6d.; morocco, gilt edges, 1/0.

Large type edition. Cloth, 1/0; roan, 1/6; morocco, 2/0.

Lancashire Sunday School Songs.

    A selection of 135 Valuable and Popular Pieces, particularly adapted for Sunday School Classes. 650th thousand. Edited by the Rev. J. Compston. New edition. In paper, 1d.; cloth, 2d.; cloth, gilt, 3d.

The Penny Union Hymn Book.

    A selection of 135 Standard Pieces, intended for use in the Prayer Meeting, the Fireside Circle, &c., &c.; edited by the Rev. Nicholas Bishop, M.A. Paper, 1d; cloth, 2d.

Hymns for the Earnest.

    By John Prior. 400 original Pieces. Cloth, 6d.

Pamphlets and Books Printed and Published advantageously, through an extensive connection with the local Booksellers, and arrangements with several first-class London Publishers. Terms, Estimates, and Specimens may be had on application.

Religious and Temperance Book and Tract Depot,
11, MARKET STREET, MANCHESTER.

.

CPSIA information can be obtained at www.ICGtesting.com
Printed in the USA
BVOW07s1723130314

347580BV00007B/147/P

9 781279 155011